The author

THE
REVOLUTION
OF 1911

A GREAT DEMOCRATIC REVOLUTION OF CHINA

WU YU-CHANG

FOREIGN LANGUAGES PRESS

PEKING 1964

First Edition   1962
Second Edition   1963
Third Edition (Revised translation) 1964

PUBLISHER'S NOTE

October 10, 1961 marks the 50th anniversary of the Revolution of 1911. The present English edition has been prepared to commemorate this great Chinese revolution and give our foreign readers a better understanding of it. The book will help them to comprehend why this revolution took place at that time in China, what it achieved and why it failed.

For the benefit of our readers a number of footnotes have been added.

Printed in the People's Republic of China

CONTENTS

ON THE REVOLUTION OF 1911

1

Speaking of the historical significance of the democratic revolution carried out by the Chinese people after the revolution of the Taiping Heavenly Kingdom,[1] Mao Tse-tung points out explicitly, "The Revolution of 1911 was the beginning of that revolution in a fuller sense."[2] It was a revolution of great historical significance during the period of democratic revolution in China. It overthrew the Ching Dynasty, ended the system of absolute monarchy which had lasted for more than two thousand years in China, gave birth to the Republic of China, intensified the Chinese people's consciousness of democracy, and gave impetus to their revolutionary struggle.

From the middle of the 19th century China underwent a tortuous and complex process of transformation. All the social, political and ideological changes which took place dur-

---

[1] The War of the Taiping Heavenly Kingdom was a peasant revolutionary war waged against the feudal rule and national oppression of the Ching Dynasty in the middle of the 19th century. Hung Hsiu-chuan, Yang Hsiu-ching and others, the leaders of this revolution, staged an uprising in Kwangsi in January 1851 and proclaimed the founding of the Taiping Heavenly Kingdom. In 1852 the peasant army proceeded northward from Kwangsi and marched through Hunan, Hupeh, Kiangsi and Anhwei and in 1853 it captured Nanking, the main city on the lower Yangtse. Part of its forces then continued the drive north and pushed to the vicinity of Tientsin, a major city in northern China. Because the Taiping army failed to build stable base areas in the places it occupied and also because, after establishing its capital in Nanking, the leading group in the army committed many political and military errors, it could not withstand the joint attack of the counter-revolutionary troops of the Ching government and the aggressors of Britain, the United States and France, and suffered defeat in 1864.

[2] Mao Tse-tung, *On New Democracy*, Foreign Languages Press, Peking, 1960, p. 9.

ing this period were conducive to the Revolution of 1911. Because China had been invaded by the capitalist forces from Europe and America, it was necessary for it to effect radical social reforms and adopt the capitalist system itself before it could resist these forces. The earliest bourgeois statesmen of China, like Kang Yu-wei and Liang Chi-chao, considered that such reforms could be effected by other than revolutionary means. For instance, they thought the Japanese way, which was to rely on government measures for reforms, could be adopted. But all the Ching government did was to equip the army with foreign guns and open a few factories, refusing to carry out any political reforms right down to the end of the 19th century. The coup d'etat of 1898[1] was the forcible expression by the ruling die-hards in the Ching government of its rejection of political reforms. If, at that time, it had stood firm against foreign aggression the government might have won greater support from the people. It proved itself very cowardly, and its cowardice exasperated the people. From 1899 to 1900 a struggle against foreign aggression was waged by the Yi Ho Tuan.[2] The Ching government, however, gave

---

[1] At the end of the 19th century intellectuals represented by Kang Yu-wei and Liang Chi-chao launched a movement for bourgeois political reform. They demanded that the system of absolute monarchy be replaced by a constitutional monarchy and hoped that Emperor Kuang Hsu would use his power to introduce political reforms. In 1898 the emperor accepted their proposals and issued a series of decrees authorizing the reforms. But this work was soon stopped by the die-hards represented by the Empress Dowager, who put the emperor under house arrest and took over the reins of government herself. Tan Sze-tung and five other reformers were executed, while Kang Yu-wei and Liang Chi-chao went into exile abroad. Later the reformers continued to support the emperor and a constitutional monarchy and became a reactionary faction in direct opposition to the bourgeois and petty-bourgeois revolutionaries led by Sun Yat-sen.

[2] Yi Ho Tuan (Society of Righteousness and Harmony) was a secret society in northern China, which was formed by peasants and handicraftsmen and was based upon superstitious cults. In 1900 it waged an armed struggle against imperialism which soon developed into an extensive, spontaneous mass movement. For details see pp. 45-52.

it no effective support. What is more, after the occupation of Peking by the allied forces of the eight powers,[1] the Ching government signed the humiliating Protocol of 1901, granting the eight imperialist countries the privilege of stationing troops in China, and promising to pay an indemnity of 450 million taels of silver, a debt amounting to 980 million taels inclusive of interest. This colossal debt was to be discharged in thirty-nine years, the security being the revenue from the customs and salt taxes. The collection of these taxes was to be carried out under foreign supervision. China was not only directly menaced by the armed forces of the imperialist powers but also subjected to their interference in its revenue and expenditure, and forced deeper and deeper into the abyss of a semi-colony.

The Protocol of 1901 aroused great anger amongst the people. Dr. Sun Yat-sen, the great revolutionary democrat, said that, previously when he advocated the revolutionary cause he was looked upon as a dangerous person and very few people dared to associate with him. After the signing of the protocol many sympathized with him and an ever increasing number of people stated that they were in favour of a revolution. Why then this change? The heightening of the patriotic spirit of the broad masses was naturally an important cause. But why at that particular time did so many people sympathize with the idea of the democratic revolution advocated by Dr. Sun Yat-sen? It was because a new social foundation had been laid. This social foundation was the bourgeoisie, a new-born class. Capitalists emerged in China

---

[1] In 1900 eight imperialist powers, Britain, France, Japan, tsarist Russia, Germany, the United States, Italy and Austria, sent a joint force to attack China in an attempt to suppress the Yi Ho Tuan Uprising of the Chinese people against aggression. The Chinese people resisted heroically. The allied forces of the eight powers captured Taku and occupied Tientsin and Peking. Subsequently, the Ching government concluded the Protocol of 1901 with the eight imperialist countries.

in the eighties and the nineties of the 19th century. At the turn of the 20th century, they were beginning to become a class.

Let us now look at the growth of the industry run by national capitalists in this period. Before 1900 there were only 122 private manufacturing and mining enterprises with an investment of over 10,000 silver dollars each, the total amount of their investment being 22.77 million silver dollars. By 1906 the number of enterprises had increased to 136, their total investments having risen to 27 million silver dollars. The development of the cotton textile industry is specially worthy of attention. In 1896 there were only 12 cotton mills in the whole country. Seven of them were owned by Chinese. The total number of spindles in these 12 mills was 417,000 of which 259,000 belonged to Chinese mills. The total number of looms was 2,100, and of these 1,750 were in Chinese-owned mills. The textile industry at that time was most highly developed in Shanghai and Kiangsu. In 1902 there were 17 cotton mills in Shanghai alone with a total of 565,000 spindles. In 1908 there were 23 cotton mills in Kiangsu, with 587,000 spindles and 3,066 looms. The silk reeling industry had also made marked progress. In 1895 there were 12 filatures in Shanghai. By 1903 the number of filatures had doubled and the number of reels was 8,526. In 1909 there were 35 filatures in Shanghai with a total of 11,085 reels. In 1911 the number of filatures was increased to 48 and that of reels to 13,738. Furthermore, many other industries, such as flour milling, the manufacture of matches, cement, tobacco, glass, and machine tools, had also developed.

The development of these capitalist enterprises was far from being sufficient to meet the needs. It was precisely because of this insufficiency that the bourgeoisie desired further development, increasingly resented the menace of foreign capital, and became more concerned about political reform. Take the building of railways for example. Before the Sino-Japanese War[1] the Chinese people were unaware of the urgent need for railways. But after that war, prompted by foreigners, and also because of their own awakening, they began to realize the need for railways. Consequently at the turn of the century, they began to build them on a large scale. The Ching government, weighed down by debts and hard put to find any money for such a purpose, decided to solicit loans from foreign countries. In 1896 it set up a railway company and appointed Sheng Hsuan-huai, a big pro-U.S. comprador, as its director. Sheng wanted to borrow money from the United States and employ American engineers to build railways. At that time the imperialist powers were scrambling madly for seaports and spheres of influence in China, and investment in railways was one means whereby they could consolidate their power. The appeal for foreign loans for the building of railways created competition among the foreign powers but at the same time it also aroused extensive opposition among the Chinese people. Yu Chih-mu, a capitalist from Hunan Province, who was connected with the revolutionary movement was the president of the Chamber of Commerce and director of the Board of Education in Changsha. He was subsequently arrested by the Ching government in the summer of 1906 and condemned to the gallows in early 1907. He was one of the bourgeoisie who carried out active agitation amongst the people against the use of foreign loans for the building of railways. He consistently maintained his opinion both whilst he was president of the Chamber of Commerce

---

[1] The war broke out in 1894 as a result of Japanese aggression against Korea and her provocations to the Chinese land and naval forces. In this war the Chinese forces put up a heroic fight, but China suffered defeat owing to the corruption of the Ching government and its lack of preparation for resistance. As a result, the Ching government had to conclude the shameful Treaty of Shimonoseki with Japan, under which it ceded Taiwan and the Penghu Islands, paid war reparations of 200 million taels of silver, permitted the Japanese to set up factories in China, opened Shasi, Chungking, Soochow and Hangchow as treaty ports and recognized Korea as Japan's dependency.

and whilst he was in prison. He even made a will in which he called on the people to oppose the use of foreign loans.

At this time the voices of those demanding the restoration of China's rights were heard throughout the country. The people of Kiangsu and Chekiang succeeded in their heroic struggle to regain the right to build the Kiangsu-Hangchow-Ningpo Railway themselves and this gave encouragement to the people of the whole country. Opposition to the use of foreign loans for the opening of mines was another stormy issue stirred up by the bourgeoisie. In Shansi Province people raised funds to buy back mining rights from the British. Opposition to the use of foreign loans for the building of railways and the opening of mines was continually manifested in other provinces.

Under such circumstances, a mass patriotic movement was imminent. In the winter of 1904 and at the beginning of 1905, there was opposition to the United States demand for the renewal of the treaty, an anti-Chinese measure, prohibiting immigration of Chinese labourers into the United States. The Chinese bourgeoisie and petty bourgeoisie in opposition to this measure launched a large-scale movement for the boycott of American goods. This spread to cities, big and small, in more than ten provinces.

Some of the Chinese bourgeoisie resided in foreign countries. Many of them had originally been small merchants, some had been workers. They had few connections with the feudal ruling class in the home country. Having come into contact with Western bourgeois culture and having been discriminated against by the foreigners, they were highly dissatisfied with the corrupt and impotent Ching government. It was natural for them to entertain revolutionary sentiments.

It was among the overseas Chinese bourgeoisie that Dr. Sun Yat-sen's activities began. Dr. Sun came from a peasant family though his upbringing, strictly speaking, was not that of a peasant. His elder brother who went to Honolulu when he was young, raised stock there, and made quite a fortune. While

8

still a boy Sun Yat-sen went to Honolulu and, supported by his brother, started school there. Thus it may be said that he came from a bourgeois background. Seventy-eight per cent of the members of the Hsing Chung Hui (the Society for the Revival of China), founded by Dr. Sun in 1894, were overseas Chinese and 48 per cent of them belonged to the overseas Chinese bourgeoisie. The armed uprisings which Dr. Sun launched in the coastal regions in later times were all supported by funds contributed by overseas Chinese.

From what has been said above, it is easy to see that the bourgeoisie was earnestly demanding political reforms. But the bourgeoisie was not the only revolutionary class. Besides, it was still very weak. The revolutionaries had confidence in the success of revolution mainly because the broad masses of the people were revolutionary-minded.

Social conditions in China during the period 1903-11 reflected the disastrous results of the invasion by foreign capital. The Chinese people's standard of living had been very low before the invasion of foreign capital, but many of them were still able to eke out a living by various means. The peasants, who were the bulk of the population, lived on the basis of small peasant economy. It was the age-old practice for the men to do the farm work and the women to make cloth, engaging at the same time in some side-occupations or other handicrafts. Under feudal rule, they maintained a self-sufficient economy although it was of a very low standard. During the first twenty years after the Opium War of 1840, foreigners were surprised to see most of the people living in the countryside near Shanghai and Canton still spinning and weaving by hand. But towards the end of the 19th century and at the beginning of the 20th century imported cheap machine-made cotton cloth began to flood the market, taking the place of the homespun type made in the countryside. The manufacture of such goods as silk fabrics and porcelain-ware, hitherto important export items, also declined because of the decrease in exports and an increase in imports. Under such conditions

9

the peasants and handicraftsmen found it more difficult to eke out a livelihood. The Ching government levied heavier taxes and the landlords intensified their exploitation so that the life of the common people became even more difficult. During this period the number of peasant riots increased every year. They were launched under slogans, such as "Resist the excises", "Resist taxes" and "Attack the rice-hoarders". From 1907 to 1910 more than 80 incidents occurred in the middle and lower reaches of the Yangtse River alone. The people attacked the rice-hoarders and refused to pay the excise tax. In 1910 tens of thousands of people took part in the rice riots in Changsha, Hunan. Similar mass struggles against the levying of excise taxes also took place in Laiyang, Shantung.

With the growth of capitalism the Chinese working class gradually became stronger. The Chinese workers had previous experience in revolutionary struggles. In 1906 more than 6,000 workers of the Anyuan Colliery took part in the uprisings launched by the China Revolutionary League in Pinghsiang in Kiangsi, and Liuyang and Liling in Hunan. In 1911 the building workers on the Szechuan-Hankow Railway staged an uprising in response to the bourgeoisie's movement opposing the Ching government's policy for the "nationalization of railways".[1] The workers also organized many strikes to improve their living conditions.

These great upheavals were an indication that feudal society was rapidly collapsing. Not only workers, peasants and handicraftsmen were in open revolt, but many of the comparatively enlightened landlords were worried and trying to find a way out both economically and politically. But what was the solution? The feudalists were in a blind alley, and could only pin their hopes on the bourgeoisie. This was why many of them were swept along into the political move-

---

[1] The policy was a manoeuvre meant to surrender the building of the railway to the imperialists.

ment of the bourgeoisie, becoming either followers of Dr. Sun Yat-sen or followers of Kang Yu-wei and Liang Chi-chao.

Due to the fact that more and more people in all parts of the country were clearly leaning towards revolution, small local revolutionary groups appeared one after another at the end of the 19th century and at the beginning of the 20th century. These groups were composed of members of the bourgeoisie and petty bourgeoisie together with a section of the enlightened landlords. Though differing in origin they were as one in opposition to the rule of the Ching Dynasty. In 1905, under the leadership of Dr. Sun Yat-sen, these small local groups merged and the China Revolutionary League was formed. The programme of the league was bourgeois in character. In addition to aiming at the overthrow of the Ching government it stood for the establishment of a republic and, in agreement with a proposal made by Dr. Sun Yat-sen, it added the equalization of landownership to its programme. In fact, this programme was the programme for the Revolution of 1911.

2

From what has been said above it is obvious that revolution was already gaining momentum in the decade immediately preceding the Revolution of 1911. The people found it impossible to live in the old way, and the rulers were unable to rule as they had done previously.

The people therefore favoured the revolution. The rulers tried to retard the revolution in an attempt to save themselves from the impending crisis. By the beginning of the 20th century the Ching government realized that it could no longer remain as intransigent as it was at the time of the suppression of the Reform Movement in 1898. It gradually issued a number of decrees authorizing reforms, among which were the abolition of the old system of competitive examination,[1] the opening of modern schools, sending students abroad to study, dismissing superfluous government personnel, establishing a board of commerce, and adopting a policy of protection for industries run by Chinese capitalists. These were the measures which Kang Yu-wei and his party had fought for, in vain, at the end of the 19th century. The people's demand for political reform had now gone much further, and although the Ching government did carry out a certain number of reforms, they failed to satistfy the people. The Ching government was finally compelled to agree to form a constitutional government and, in 1905, sent five ministers abroad to study constitutionalism. Three years later it announced that a constitutional government would be formed in 1917, after a preparatory period of nine years. In 1907 the Board of Commerce was changed into the Board of Agriculture, Industry and Commerce. Meanwhile it was announced that promoters of industry would be awarded titles. Those who invested 20 million silver dollars or over in industry would be made a viscount of the first degree and those who invested 100,000 silver dollars or over would be given an official title of the fifth grade.[2] These measures not only gave a certain amount of recognition to the political status of the bourgeoisie, but also signified that the Ching government had been compelled to make greater concession.

The reform measures promised and carried out by the Ching government intensified the disagreements among the bourgeoisie. The revolutionaries headed by Dr. Sun Yat-sen

---

[1] The competitive examination system was a method by which the feudal rulers recruited officials for government service. It was also a means of luring intellectuals into submission. The system was first adopted in the 7th century A.D. and its practice continued until the early 20th century.

[2] Under the Ching Dynasty imperial official ranks were divided into nine grades.

considered that the Ching government's measures of reform were but a subterfuge, that its promises could not even be taken at their face value, and that only by overthrowing the Ching government could a democratic system be established. But the constitutional monarchists headed by Kang Yu-wei and Liang Chi-chao, who represented the right wing of the bourgeoisie and a section of the landlords and bureaucrats, considered that although the Ching government's reforms might be only a subterfuge and that its promises could not be taken at their face value it was nevertheless possible to carry out legal struggles. They believed that it was better to strive for political reform by legal means than to suffer the pain of revolution.

Even at the time when the Ching government was opposed to any reform, the revolutionaries had already appeared and expressed different views from those held by the constitutional monarchists. Around 1905 the differences intensified and resulted in a political split among the bourgeoisie.

This split became deeper after 1909 when the Ching government set up a State Assembly in the national capital, and an assembly in each one of the provinces. They resembled the bourgeois law-making bodies such as the Parliament and Congress of the West. The State Assembly had 300 members, of which 125 were appointed by the emperor. This group was comprised of 10 peers, 5 members of the imperial clan, and 100 officials of various government boards and departments. The remaining 10 of the appointed members were men who owned properties valued at one million dollars or over. About 170 members of the State Assembly were elected from among members of the provincial assemblies. The members of the provincial assembly were in turn elected from the various counties. Persons who could stand for election included the following: Those who had done educational work or other kinds of public service for three years or more; middle school or higher institution graduates; those who had received the title of licentiate, senior licentiate, provincial graduate[1] or higher degree; those who had been civil officials of the seventh grade or above; those who had been military officers of the fifth grade or above; those who owned industrial or commercial enterprises capitalized at 5,000 silver dollars or more and those who owned landed property of the same value. There were at the time 23 provinces and regions in the country and the total number of provincial assembly members was 1,677. The provincial assemblies could discuss and pass resolutions concerning the following affairs of the province: the introduction of new measures and abolition of out-of-date practices, the budget and financial account, the taxation law, public debt, and other responsibilities. The provincial assemblies were obviously a great centre of attraction for the upper strata of the bourgeoisie. Many of them managed to get themselves elected members of the provincial assemblies and some even succeeded in becoming speakers.

The provincial assemblies, in addition to widening the split among the bourgeoisie, produced two other effects.

First, they deepened the people's sense of democracy. The provincial assemblies were law-making bodies to which many of the bourgeoisie, petty bourgeoisie and landlords who wanted reforms were elected. And they immediately became forums demanding political reform. With a rising revolutionary movement, petitions for constitutional government increased in number and vigour and the demand for political reform swiftly developed into an irresistible tide. The Ching government was forced to make further concessions. First it declared that constitutional government would begin in 1917, later it stated that it would begin in 1913, four years ahead of the original schedule. This concession failed to satisfy the people; even members of the provincial assemblies were

---

[1] Licentiate (*hsiutsai*), senior licentiate (*kungsheng*), provinical graduate (*chujen*), and metropolitan graduate (*chinshih*) were titled degrees conferred on scholars who passed different stages of the competitive examinations in feudal China.

14

disappointed with the Ching government's lack of sincerity in carrying out reforms. The movement to oppose the use of foreign loans for the building of railways launched in Szechuan, Hunan, Hupeh and Kwangtung and the movement to oppose the use of foreign loans for the opening of mines launched in Shantung, Shansi and other provinces, were started as a result of the demands made in the provincial assemblies. Because these movements were in the interests of the people, the more these questions were discussed in the provincial assemblies the greater the number of people who became involved. As the people were opposed to the Ching Dynasty, the movement which originated amongst members of the provincial assemblies soon became a mass revolutionary movement against Ching rule. The overwhelming majority of the members of the provincial assemblies were reformists and not in favour of a revolution, but they ultimately became the unconscious tools of the revolution.

Secondly, the provincial assemblies also played the dual role of dampening the revolutionary spirit of the bourgeoisie and intensifying its proneness to compromise. Most of the bourgeois members of the provincial assemblies belonged to the upper strata of the intellectuals, and no matter how urgently they demanded democratic reform in political affairs they had no desire for democratic social reforms. Now when they joined hands with the landed gentry in the provincial assemblies for political reform, they inevitably went a step further and opposed democratic social reforms. This was a situation deserving serious attention. It should be noted that prior to the Revolution of 1911 the provincial assemblies formed a strong base for the bourgeois constitutional monarchists. This fact placed the revolutionaries in an extremely disadvantageous position after the outbreak of the revolution. The revolutionaries were forced into a position secondary to that of the constitutional monarchists who were working hand in glove with the feudal force.

The role played by the provincial assemblies may be estimated as follows. Before the advent of the revolution, while they weakened the strength of the revolution they also pushed the revolutionary movement forward because of their demand for political reforms and their exposure of the corruption and incompetence of the Ching government. After the revolution began, they tried to prove they were supporters of the republican system but, by allying themselves with the feudal forces in opposition to the revolutionaries, they actually became an obstacle to the revolutionary movement.

3

The merging of local revolutionary bodies to form the China Revolutionary League marked a big step forward in the revolutionary movement. Upon careful examination it can be seen that the main result of this change was the emergence of a common programme: "Drive out the Manchus, revive the Chinese nation, establish a republic, and equalize land-ownership." In other words it meant the overthrow of the Ching government, the establishment of the Chinese Republic and equalization of landownership. Of these three principles the second and third were the great contribution made by the Revolutionary League and its leader Dr. Sun Yat-sen. Before the founding of the league those who stood for the overthrow of the Ching Dynasty had always used the slogan of the "restoration of the Ming Dynasty"[1] or the "founding of a Han empire". In 1894 Hsing Chung Hui (the Society for the Revival of China) included in its programme a call for the establishment of a "united government". What was meant by this "united government"? It may have been derived from

_____

[1] The Ming Dynasty (1368-1644) was reigned by the feudal ruling class of the Han people, the majority nationality of China. The Ching Dynasty (1644-1911) was set up by the rulers of the Manchu people in China.

the term "the United States of America". If so, it would mean a federated government which was of course a form of bourgeois republican government. Thus it can be seen that at the time the Society for the Revival of China was active the people still did not have definite revolutionary ideas. What China urgently needed at that time was a clear political conception of democracy. After the founding of the Revolutionary League the demand for the establishment of a republic soon became widespread and the old slogan calling for a Han empire was dropped. The programme of the Revolutionary League therefore did have a great influence upon the people.

The equalization of landownership was an entirely new ideal. This ideal showed that the Chinese bourgeoisie, who were not so advanced as the bourgeoisie of the West, hoped that their republic would become permanent through the establishment of good relations with the peasants and that it would not be overthrown by another revolution.

But which one of the Revolutionary League's three principles was most important in the minds of the people? It was certainly not the equalization of landownership, nor was it the establishment of a republic. It goes without saying that the immediate aim of the revolutionaries was to overthrow the Ching government. The question is why did they want to overthrow it. Was it for the purpose of establishing a Chinese republic? Certainly many people supported a republic, and most of them were bourgeois revolutionaries. However a far greater number of people favoured the revolution simply because they did not like the Ching government. Such people could be found amongst all classes. They hated the Ching government not only because it was corrupt and incompetent, and had brought disasters upon the nation but mainly because it was controlled by Manchu noblemen who carried out a strict policy of racial discrimination. Some people went so far as to say that the Ching government had to be overthrown even if it did carry out democratic reforms. The bourgeoisie took advantage of the people's hatred of Ching rule and promoted the idea of

17

revolution. There was nothing wrong in this, but the level of understanding of the bourgeois revolutionaries at that time differed little from that of the ordinary people. Their propaganda left only two deep impressions. One was that they were against the Manchus and the other that they took pride in the glorious heritage left by their Han ancestors. This kind of propaganda produced a tremendous effect and it was mainly this which raised the storm of revolution. However it also had serious shortcomings. The anti-Manchu propaganda was much too simple. It concentrated all the hatred on the Manchu rulers, was tinged with the racial sentiments of the Han people, and therefore did not raise the national consciousness of the people. As the result of this propaganda the real enemy of the Chinese people, the foreign aggressors, was ignored. Similarly, the propaganda about the glorious heritage of the Hans was also oversimplified. It failed to make any critical analysis and to oppose Han feudalism which dominated China for many centuries, and it ignored an arch internal enemy, the Han feudal forces which had supported the Ching rule. It is true that before the Revolution of 1911 the revolutionaries carried on a great deal of political agitation and devoted considerable effort to enlightening the people, but owing to their oversimplification of the task and lack of adequate theoretical explanation they failed to storm the ideological fortress of feudalism. Furthermore, they failed to make any creative efforts in the theoretical realm. They also neglected to introduce into China, in a systematic way, the writings of Western scholars of the Enlightenment in the 17th and 18th centuries and those of the great thinkers of the middle 19th century. Actually many foreign classical works now being translated and published in China should have been translated by bourgeois scholars before the 1911 Revolution. The serious weakness of the Revolution of 1911 was that it lacked an ideological revolution to pave the way.

It must be understood, however, that these revolutionaries, who were strongly imbued with the idea of opposing the Manchus, are worthy of great respect. They were full of enthusiasm and noble sentiments, and ready to give their lives, if need be, in the struggle to overthrow the Ching rule. Their spirit of self-sacrifice has left an indelible impression on the Chinese people.

It should be noted that these brave people did not always join in concerted action. Among the small groups which later merged into the Revolutionary League, for instance, there was an organization called the Kuang Fu Hui (the Restoration Society). Some of its members refused to join the Revolutionary League and acted independently. Among them was Hsu Hsi-lin, the famous revolutionary who assassinated En Ming, the Ching governor of Anhwei, and became a historic figure. There were also people who joined the Revolutionary League for a while and then advocated separation. The famous scholar Chang Tai-yen was such a man. He was chief editor of the *Min Pao* (*People's Journal*), the organ of the Revolutionary League. In 1909 he suddenly distributed leaflets attacking Dr. Sun Yat-sen, and after the Revolution of 1911 he severed his relations with the Revolutionary League and organized another party.

Dr. Sun Yat-sen played an active role in leading the armed uprisings. It was his opinion that the Ching Dynasty in the beginning of the 20th century already resembled a ramshackle house and that the removal of a single beam or cornerstone would cause the whole structure to collapse. This was why, after the founding of the Revolutionary League, his revolutionary activities, including attempts to win over the secret societies[1] and the raising of funds, were designed for the pur-

---

[1] The secret societies and religious sects mentioned later in this book such as the Society of Brothers, Big Sword Society, Red Lantern Sect, were backward, primitive forms of people's organizations in feudal China, based on some religious tenet or superstitious practice. The members were mainly recruited from among bankrupt peasants, unemployed handicraftsmen and *lumpen* proletarians. The variously named societies were of patriarchal pattern, and some possessed arms. Through these organizations the *lumpen* proletarians sought to help each other

pose of launching uprisings. The uprisings led by him however were not based on patient work among the masses, but rather upon military adventurism, hence their failure one after another. Dr. Sun Yat-sen organized a number of armed "dare-to-die" corps to make sudden raids on selected coastal regions and on certain places in the southwest which were garrisoned by Ching troops. They received no outside help, no aid from the local people, and the work of liaison was badly arranged. Every one of the raids ended in failure. In 1910, after the uprising staged by the new army of Canton had failed, the most active leaders of the uprising felt downcast and discouraged because of the great losses suffered. At that time conditions in the country were becoming increasingly favourable for revolution. Would it not be regrettable if no continuous efforts were made to push the revolution forward? Dr. Sun Yat-sen together with Huang Hsing and other leaders of the Revolutionary League succeeded in finding a solution to the problem. They decided to concentrate their forces upon preparing and launching a decisive uprising in Canton. This was the famous campaign launched on April 27, 1911. It also became known as the Huanghuakang Campaign (because the martyrs were buried by the people in Huanghuakang, Canton). The old methods were used to launch this uprising. Members of the Revolutionary League were called to Canton from various provinces and a "dare-to-die" corps composed of more than 800 men was organized. Some 700 rifles and 300 bombs were smuggled into the city and 40 centres were set up. Many of the members of the corps wrote their last words. They staked everything upon a single throw. The uprising failed. Nevertheless, it had a salutary effect. It encouraged the people and

---

socially and economically and on occasions fought their oppressors, the bureaucrats and landlords. However, because they were backward and had no constructive policy they could not solve the problems of the peasants and handicraftsmen. Furthermore, they often degenerated into the tools of the landlords and bureaucrats and turned into reactionary bodies.

alarmed the corrupt, incompetent officials of the Ching government, who were at a loss to know how to deal with the revolution.

The Revolutionary League suffered greatly from the failure of the uprising. It lost many excellent cadres which weakened the forces of the revolution. And what was worse, the leadership of the league was lost. Although Dr. Sun Yat-sen was still working in the United States among overseas Chinese and trying to raise funds to prepare for new uprisings he gave no actual leadership to the league. Chao Sheng, the famous league activist, became ill after the failure of the Canton Uprising and died in Hongkong not long afterwards. Huang Hsing became pessimistic and did not know what to do next. A group of league members led by Sung Chiao-jen set up the Central China Headquarters of the Revolutionary League in Shanghai. Although nominally a branch of the Revolutionary League, it was actually an independent body established because of dissatisfaction with the leadership of the league.

It could hardly be expected that a revolutionary body, plagued by dissension and disunity even before the revolution, would be able to maintain a united front after victory.

4

It was not a matter of chance that the Revolution of 1911 broke out in Wuchang. Revolutionary organizations appeared there as early as 1904. Some of their members had consistently carried out the work of agitation and organization among the rank and file of the Ching army. Two revolutionary organizations existed in Wuchang prior to the Revolution of 1911, the Wen Hsueh Sheh (the Literary Association), and a branch of the Kung Chin Hui (the Society for Mutual Progress). The latter, a merger of a number of the secret societies in various provinces, was set up by league members as a front organization for the Revolutionary League. The new army of Hupeh

Province consisted of 16,000 men. More than 5,000 of them joined the Literary Association and quite a number of them joined the Society for Mutual Progress. The new army came completely under the influence of these two organizations, a general command was established and preparations were made for an uprising. Later the headquarters of the command was raided, a number of its leading members were arrested and murdered, others were able to get away and go into hiding. However, since most of the soldiers had become revolutionaries and there was such a strong desire for an insurrection that even without leadership an uprising was successfully launched and the first victory of the revolution was scored.

Because the uprising was launched without leadership, the soldiers after their initial victory were confronted with many unforeseen difficulties. The first problem they had to solve was the establishment of a government with an authoritative head. At that time the people did not realize that after the seizure of power they themselves should become the rulers. They looked for someone outside their own ranks and then offered the reins of government to that person. On the eve of the uprising, the soldiers had seized a company commander and forced him to be their leader. When they later wanted him to organize a government he refused to do so under any circumstance. The soldiers had to look for another man. Finally their choice fell on Tang Hua-lung, a constitutional monarchist and speaker of the provincial assembly. He was a civil official and quite unable to give leadership to the army, so it was necessary to find a military officer who could do the job. They chose Li Yuan-hung, brigade commander of the Hupeh new army, and tried to compel him at bayonet point to be governor-general of the Hupeh Military Government. He refused to comply and the soldiers locked him up. Meanwhile, the soldiers used his name and issued a declaration putting him in a compromising position. Li Yuan-hung, however, remained silent, because he wanted to be prepared for any sudden change that might occur. If the revolution failed he could then say that the revolutionaries had forced him to take action. When the situation changed for the better, a few days later, he consented to become the leader of the revolutionary government. To think that such a man should become a "distinguished founder" of the Chinese Republic!

After Li Yuan-hung and Tang Hua-lung took up their posts in the revolutionary government, all their friends naturally followed suit. The power of these men grew greater and greater while that of the real founders of the republic, the soldiers who staged the uprising and the bourgeois revolutionaries, became less and less. The soldiers were in the worst position and some of them were murdered. The veteran revolutionaries who had been active in Hupeh felt broken-hearted whenever they thought of this.

Originally, the Revolutionary League had thought that after the success in Wuchang, the troops would be sent from one place to another until they had taken the whole country. Things turned out quite differently from what had been anticipated. Practically all the places which came over to the side of the revolution did so simply by proclamation. In less than two months after the Wuchang Uprising most of the provinces and regions in the country had declared their independence of the Ching government. A general survey shows that they usually became independent in one of the following ways:

The first was patterned after the proceedings in Wuchang. The main event was an uprising staged by soldiers of the new army. After the uprising, owing to the lack of strong leadership, the political power fell into the hands of the constitutional monarchists — the upper strata of the bourgeoisie. Then the constitutional monarchists brought in the feudal forces to take charge of the government. That was how Shensi Province became independent.

The second pattern was that the masses stood up and revolted under the leadership of the bourgeois revolutionaries. After the victory of the revolt the revolutionaries actually took control of the government. Then the constitutional monarchists and the feudal forces staged a coup d'etat and overthrew the new government. This was how Hunan became independent. The soldiers of the new army staged an uprising and were led by the revolutionaries. They then killed the officers of the garrison battalion and took control of the government themselves. But immediately afterwards the constitutional monarchists staged a coup d'etat and killed all the revolutionaries, after which they and the feudal forces took over the powers of government. Kweichow also became independent in the same way as Hunan.

The third pattern was that, before a popular uprising broke out, the local constitutional monarchists would take advantage of the tense situation created by the people of the lower strata and compel the Ching officials to declare the province independent. As a result, in spite of the declaration of independence, the government remained in the hands of the old Ching officials. This pattern was followed by many provinces. Take for instance Cheng Teh-chuan, governor of Kiangsu Province. Many people persuaded him to declare the independence of the province. He simply held a meeting and changed his original title of *Hsun-fu* (governor) into the new title of *Tu-tu* (military governor). The personnel of his office remained the same. The change was in name only.

Under the fourth pattern, as used in Yunnan, a war broke out between the new and old armies, after which the new army drove away the old rulers and a new regime was set up.

In Szechuan, there was another pattern, and conditions became much more complicated. After May 1911, because the Ching government accepted foreign loans and took over the Szechuan-Hankow Railway line which was to have been built with local funds, it aroused strong opposition among the broad masses in Szechuan. The building of the Szechuan-Hankow Railway was originally proposed by the people of Szechuan in order to resist inroads by Western countries. The fund for building the railway was raised by the "rent share" method. Under this arrangement, 3 per cent of all the collected land rents was set apart as shares in the railway. Thus every one of the 60 or 70 million people in the province, both rich and poor, became economically connected with the building of the railway. A movement to protect the railway rights was first led by members of the provincial assembly which was dominated by constitutional monarchists. To strengthen their struggle they organized the Association for the Protection of Railway Rights, making use of the Society of Brothers of Szechuan which had a broad popular basis. The Society of Brothers was a secret society, the real aim of which was to overthrow the Ching and restore the Ming Dynasty. Backed by the provincial assembly it openly carried out various activities. The members of the Revolutionary League and the Society for Mutual Progress had been carrying out their work in the Society of Brothers for many years, and the constitutional monarchists were unable to control the movement to protect the railway rights as it grew in strength. The scope and influence of the movement was exceedingly wide. Workers, peasants, students, and people of other social strata, in more than 100 sub-prefectures and counties all joined the movement, held demonstrations and strikes. On September 7, Chao Erh-feng, governor-general of Szechuan, ordered a massacre of the people in Chengtu, who had petitioned against the acceptance of foreign loans. This made the people of Szechuan more indignant, and the people of the counties rose en masse to support the people of Chengtu. Besieged, Chao Erh-feng could do nothing but wait for help. The Ching government ordered Tuan Fang, imperial commissioner for the building of the Canton-Hankow and Szechuan-Hankow Railways, to go to Szechuan to suppress the people. Tuan Fang took with him a contingent of the new army of Hupeh, but they had established connections with members of the Revolutionary League at Wanhsien and Neikiang, staged an uprising at Tzechow and killed Tuan Fang. Following this, members of the Revolutionary League staged an uprising at Neikiang and other counties. By this time a part of the new army of Szechuan had also launched an uprising in the vicinity of Chengtu and had begun to march to Chungking. Joining forces with the members of the Revolutionary League there they occupied Chungking and established the Szechuan Military Government, making Chang Pei-chueh, a member of the league, military governor of the province. Chao Erh-feng saw that the situation was hopeless as far as he was concerned, and transferred his powers to Pu Tien-chun, a constitutional monarchist and speaker of the provincial assembly. The latter then set up the "Great Han Military Government of Szechuan" in Chengtu. This created a situation with governments in both Chengtu and Chungking opposed to each other. Later the Chungking party surrendered to the Chengtu party and the political power fell into the hands of the feudal force.

In conclusion, it may be pointed out that although the procedure to attain independence varied, the result was nearly always the same.

Why did things turn out like this? It was because the revolutionaries were not strong enough. Hoping for an early success of the revolution, they were willing to co-operate with everyone who professed republicanism. In the scramble for power, carried out under the name of the republic, the winner, so long as he professed support of republicanism, went scot-free even though he had the blood of revolutionaries on his hands. The revolutionaries had great confidence in the republican system, thinking that it could ensure the status of the bourgeoisie. They did not foresee the possibility of any differences arising between themselves and other supporters of the republic after the victory of the revolution. Thus when the various political parties vied with each other to expand their influence the revolutionaries did not understand it was necessary to increase their own power.

Things were different with the constitutional monarchists. While on the one hand they did all they could to pass themselves off as ardent supporters of the republican system, on the other hand, they never forgot that there were political differences between themselves and the revolutionaries. They kept a sharp eye on the latter to avoid being excluded by them. The constitutional monarchists knew that they were weak too. They sought to squeeze out the revolutionaries and to avoid being squeezed out themselves. In an attempt to consolidate their own position the constitutional monarchists strove to form an alliance with the feudal force, for the purpose of opposing the revolutionaries. In short, although the revolutionaries tried to conciliate the constitutional monarchists, the latter refused to unite with them. The result was that the bourgeoisie remained politically divided all the way through.

Under such conditions it was no wonder that Yuan Shih-kai took the place of Sun Yat-sen, that the provisional government of Peking took the place of the Provisional Government of Nanking,[1] and that the old forces took the place of the new forces which had grown up in the course of the revolution.

From what has been stated it can be seen that the important reasons for the failure of the Revolution of 1911 were the lack of preparation and errors in leadership with regard to the fundamental problems of revolutionary theory, revolutionary organization, the revolutionary armed forces and revolutionary government. This provides a grim historical lesson. In evaluating the Revolution of 1911, however, it would be incorrect to see only its shortcomings and consider

---

[1] Following the victory of the Wuchang Uprising on October 10, 1911, one province after another responded with a declaration of independence. Then on January 1, 1912, the provinces which had declared themselves independent set up the Provisional Government in Nanking, electing Dr. Sun Yat-sen as the provisional president. At that time the military power of the Ching government was in the hands of the warlord Yuan Shih-kai, then in Peking, who wanted to overthrow both the Ching emperor and the revolution and to usurp the fruits of the revolution for himself. Later, the Nanking group effected a compromise with Yuan Shih-kai and, after Yuan had forced the Ching emperor to abdicate and had announced his own "support" of the republic, they elected him to the provisional presidency. Yuan then organized a provisional government in Peking.

it only as a revolution which ended in failure. Many things would be incomprehensible if it were looked upon in this manner.

It must be admitted that although the Revolution of 1911 failed to wipe out feudalism completely it gave feudalism a fatal blow, because it overthrew the Ching rule and ended the system of absolute monarchy in China. For a long period of time and to a great extent the system of absolute monarchy accounted for the continued existence of feudalism. The supreme authority of the system of absolute monarchy actually meant the supreme authority of feudalism. The absolute monarchy did not allow any violation of feudalism and hence it long remained a serious barrier to social progress. The removal of this barrier made democracy an irresistible tide. Formerly the emperor called himself the "Son of Heaven". If anyone had then said that the emperor was a robber and should be overthrown he would have been considered a lunatic. Dr. Sun Yat-sen himself was once considered to be a lunatic, but after the Revolution of 1911 the tables were turned and if anyone wanted to put the clock back and become emperor or wanted to help another man to become emperor he was considered to be a lunatic. After the Revolution of 1911 Yuan Shih-kai wanted to become emperor, and later on the warlord Chang Hsun tried to help the last emperor of the Ching Dynasty to regain his throne. Both Yuan and Chang were backed by armed forces and were confident of their success. When the time came for a show-down they soon discovered that of all those who used to support them, only a handful of their closest attendants and certain daydreamers like themselves were left.

The overthrow of the system of absolute monarchy was therefore the great achievement of the 1911 Revolution. The people saw this system collapse under their very eyes and were happy beyond words. Both the bourgeoisie and petty bourgeoisie considered that the victory of the revolution meant the beginning of a new life. For instance, after the Wuchang

28

Uprising many political parties sprang up which vied with each other in attempts to participate in the government. Looking back, many of their activities now appear rather childish, but it cannot be denied that they reflected the mounting spirit of democracy. Especially is this true of the people's cheerful and enthusiastic welcome for the victorious revolution which created a new atmosphere. Lenin was loud in praise of such a new atmosphere. He said in an article entitled "The Awakening of Asia" written in 1913:

> Was it so long ago that China was considered a typical land of unmitigated stagnation? Now China is a land of seething political activity, the scene of a virile public movement and democratic upsurge.[1]

Had it not been for the overthrow of the absolute monarchy by revolution, the appearance of this new atmosphere would have been impossible.

The Revolution of 1911 overthrew the system of absolute monarchy and established the Chinese Republic, but, owing to the inherent weakness of the Chinese bourgeoisie, it failed to fulfil the tasks of the bourgeois-democratic revolution. That is, it failed to destroy the foundation of feudalism and, most important of all, to shoulder the great responsibility of fighting against imperialism. The failure of the Revolution of 1911 made the May 4 Movement[2] inevitable. Having had the experience of this failure, the people became wiser and realized that only by overthrowing imperialism and feudalism could

---

[1] V. I. Lenin, *The National-Liberation Movement in the East*, Foreign Languages Publishing House, Moscow, 1957, p. 59.

[2] On May 4, 1919, the students of Peking held a demonstration to protest against the proposed terms of the Versailles Peace Treaty under which the imperialist countries — Britain, the United States, France, Japan and Italy — intended to give many of China's rights in Shantung Province to Japan. This movement of the students met with an instantaneous response in all parts of the country. After June 3 of the same year it became a nation-wide, anti-imperialist and anti-feudal revolutionary movement with the wide participation of the proletariat, the urban petty bourgeoisie and the national bourgeoisie.

China find a way out. A new revolutionary theory was needed and a new revolutionary path had to be found to carry out this task. By that time capitalism had made further progress in China and the proletariat had steadily grown to a strong force. Under the influence of the Great October Socialist Revolution, Chinese progressives entertained a new hope for the liberation of their nation and began to study Marxism-Leninism, thus paving the way for the May 4 Movement. The achievement of the Revolution of 1911 also made the May 4 Movement inevitable, because having experienced a great upheaval, the people were in consequence considerably emancipated both in spirit and in thought. They now dared to raise questions which they had not dared to raise before the Revolution of 1911 and were now more susceptible to the new revolutionary theories. Therefore we say that the Revolution of 1911 was an old democratic revolution led by the bourgeoisie in modern China which had great historic significance. It blazed the trail for the revolutionary cause of the Chinese people.

MEMOIRS ON
EVENTS BETWEEN THE SINO-JAPANESE WAR
OF 1894 AND THE REVOLUTION OF 1911

1. CHINA'S TRAGIC DEFEAT IN THE SINO-JAPANESE WAR OF 1894

After the invasion of China by world capitalism, the corrupt feudal society gradually disintegrated and China became a semi-colony. China could no longer close its doors to foreigners. Even staunch defenders of feudalism such as Tseng Kuo-fan, Hu Lin-yi and Li Hung-chang, who massacred the revolutionaries of the Taiping Heavenly Kingdom, thought that China had to undergo some changes in order to adapt itself to the world situation. When Hu Lin-yi saw foreign gunboats sailing swiftly up and down China's great rivers he was amazed and said that China's military equipment was outdated, that it must follow the example of the West and have gunboats and big cannons. Li Hung-chang and other feudal bureaucrats then started the movement to "learn from the foreigners". This movement began in the sixties of the 19th century, even earlier than the "modernization" carried out by Emperor Mutsuhito of Japan. But China's movement to "learn from the foreigners" was different from the modernization of Japan. Japan went through the process of modernization and took the path to capitalism. China's movement did not encourage the development of capitalism. All it wanted to do was to use Western weapons for the defence of feudal rule. That was why China remained in its backward state while Japan became wealthy and strong and, in 1894, dared to start a large-scale, aggressive war against China. In this war the Chinese people resisted Japanese aggression with great determination and their troops fought heroically. The corruption and incompetence of China's ruling circle and the sabotage of officials who wished to capitulate were responsible for China suffering a tragic defeat and losing the war. The

Ching government was compelled to send Li Hung-chang, China's arch traitorous diplomat to Japan where he signed the Treaty of Shimonoseki. By this treaty China lost both a friendly neighbour in Korea and its own territory of Taiwan. Furthermore, China had to cede the Liaotung Peninsula and open Shasi, Chungking, Soochow and Hangchow to foreign trade. Japan also obtained the right to set up factories in all the treaty ports and China had to pay the fabulous amount of 200 million taels of silver as indemnity. This unheard-of humiliating treaty spelt ruin to China. It was a shock to the people of the whole country. Previously China had only been defeated by big Western countries but now it was defeated by a small Eastern one. The defeat was disastrous and the treaty contained the most humiliating conditions. Li Hung-chang's movement to "learn from the foreigners" was an utter failure and his traitorous character was now completely exposed. All the people were against Li Hung-chang and other capitulators. At that time the metropolitan examination was about to be held and a large number of provincial graduates were in Peking. They held meetings and sent petitions to the government. Kang Yu-wei was particularly active among them. He sent a petition signed by more than a thousand provincial graduates to Emperor Kuang Hsu, demanding that the government reject the terms of such a degrading peace, move the capital, and carry out reforms to enable the country to become strong. I still remember when the news of China's defeat in the Sino-Japanese War of 1894 spread to my home town in Junghsien County, Szechuan; my elder brother, Wu Yung-kun, and I were so upset that we cried bitterly. My mother had just died and we were staying at home for the mourning period. Misfortune in the family made us feel the danger to our nation all the more keenly. Our grief was so great that no words could express it.

After the Sino-Japanese War of 1894 the imperialists rapidly increased their investments in China. This, to some degree, stimulated national capitalism. In addition, the Ching government felt compelled to make some concession to the national capitalists, because the movement to "learn from the foreigners" had failed. National capitalism was thus able to make some initial headway in China. The bourgeois ideas of the West began to spread widely in China and the political movement of the bourgeoisie gradually developed. After the Sino-Japanese War, Kang Yu-wei and Liang Chi-chao gradually became active in an endeavour to introduce bourgeois reformist ideas. At the same time Dr. Sun Yat-sen and his party also started their political activities to promote a bourgeois revolution. Meanwhile, my own thoughts following the surging tide of new ideas also underwent a change.

Before the Sino-Japanese War of 1894 my ideas were still dominated by the traditional ideas of loyalty to the emperor, filial piety, moral integrity and uprightness. In 1892, when I was 13 years old, I went with my elder brother to Chengtu and entered the Tsunching Academy. This gave me a new horizon. Among my schoolmates was a boy named Huang Chih. He obtained his licentiate degree in the same examination as my brother. He was the son of a wood-block engraver and was not looked upon with much respect by other students, but we became intimate friends. He was my senior, well read and well versed in semantics and research in Chinese classics. We often went together to visit the temple erected to Chukeh Liang and to the Tu Fu Memorial Shrine.[1] We usually took a walk on the city rampart every evening and he would point out the places of historical interest or tell me stories about Chukeh Liang and Tu Fu. Sometimes he talked about the

---

[1] Chukeh Liang (181-234) was a famous statesman and military strategist of the Three Kingdoms Period (221-265). In Chinese folklore he is represented as a paragon of wisdom and resourcefulness. To commemorate him the people in many parts of China have erected temples in his honour. Tu Fu (712-770) was a great Chinese poet of the realist school. His late years were spent in Chengtu, Szechuan. According to tradition the Tu Fu Memorial Shrine was built at the place where he once lived.

national crisis and expressed deep concern over the destiny of China. In this way during the days of my youth, I became interested in national affairs. My older schoolmates also often related how former students of the school had carried out struggles against the feudal bureaucrats. Although I did not study very long in the Tsunching Academy it left a very deep impression on my mind.

In the summer of 1892, when my mother died, my brother and I returned home. My brother was deeply imbued with the doctrine of filial piety. Every night he slept in a hut by my mother's grave which was near the house. This practice, according to the feudal code of ethics, should have lasted for three years. We would do some reading before he left for the hut. The books we read were the *General History of China* and the *One Hundred Essays of the Tien Chi and Chung Cheng Periods*. When we read the stories of the national heroes Yueh Fei,[1] Wen Tien-hsiang[2] and others we felt greatly moved and even shed a few tears. We were particularly fond of the story of Huang Chun-yao, a martyr of the late Ming Dynasty. When the Ching troops were about to capture Chiating he told his wife and younger brother to hang themselves, saying, "Brother, you go first and I'll come after you very soon." Then he calmly hanged himself. Once he wrote an essay entitled "One Is a Coward If One Does Not Do What Is Right". It contains the following passage:

> Weakness is a matter of temperament and . . . fear is the result of habit. . . . Both of these are due to a lack of courage. It is impossible to expect a man who lacks courage to keep his word and sacrifice his life in a dignified manner.

Among the scholars of the late Ming Dynasty there were heroes like Huang Chun-yao and there were also cowards like

---

[1] 1103-1141.

[2] 1236-1282.

Wu Mei-tsun, who surrendered to the Ching Dynasty. Fearing that history might record him as a traitor, however, Wu regretted what he had done. Before his death he wrote a poem which contains these lines:

> *Many of my friends were noble-minded and died*
> *as martyrs.*
> *But I was too irresolute and sought to live in shame.*
> . . . .
> *Alas! It is not easy to abandon one's wife and*
> *children;*
> *And I'm now an entirely worthless man with a blot*
> *upon my name.*

This poem reveals the agony of a man who had become a coward and traitor to the people. With regard to these two men, Wu Mei-tsun and Huang Chun-yao, an old saying is opportune: "A moment's vacillation and one sinks into oblivion for ever; a moment's perseverance and one wins everlasting glory." Whether they could stand the test or not at a critical moment determined the two entirely different ways in which history dealt with these two men after their death. Before the Sino-Japanese War of 1894 all the books I read were of the kind mentioned above. They played a great part in the formation of my patriotic and revolutionary character. As Szechuan was far away from the cultural centre of the country and new books were not available I had no chance of acquiring any knowledge of "the new learning".[1] However, I knew the dangerous situation the country was in and worried greatly about the future of my motherland. China's defeat in the Sino-Japanese War intensified my desire for national salvation and I wanted to find a way to help save the country from ruin.

---

[1] Here "the new learning" means the culture of Western bourgeois democracy, including the social theories and natural sciences, introduced into China by progressive intellectuals after the middle of the 19th century. The term is often used in contrast to "the old learning" which means the feudal culture of China.

I knew the government was corrupt and that the official world was hopeless. I was not surprised at the failure of the "learn from the foreigners" movement, but I had no idea how China could get out of the impasse. I was in a great quandary with regard to political problems. When the ideas for reform and modernization spread by Kang Yu-wei and Liang Chi-chao were introduced to Szechuan I took to them with great enthusiasm.

2. THE SHORT-LIVED REFORM MOVEMENT

After the Sino-Japanese War of 1894 the national crisis in China deepened. The "return of Liaotung by the three nations" was no boon to our country; on the contrary it gave China endless trouble. What was meant by the "return of Liaotung by the three nations"? Originally the Treaty of Shimonoseki stipulated that China should cede the Liaotung Peninsula to Japan. This aroused the envy of imperialist Russia, which sought the aid of France and Germany for their proposal that the three countries together force Japan to "return" the Liaotung Peninsula to China. France was tsarist Russia's ally and gladly complied. Germany was also hoping to have a finger in the pie and therefore also was enthusiastic about the plan. There was a strong conflict between Britain and tsarist Russia but Britain did not like the idea of a rapidly developing Japan, and so it adopted a "neutral" attitude towards the intervention of the three imperialist powers. Thus Japan stood alone and had to yield to pressure. This did not mean that Japan was willing to be lenient to China. On the contrary, it made a strong demand and forced China to pay 30 million taels of silver to redeem the Liaotung Peninsula. This was, in short, the story of the "return of Liaotung by the three nations", an event often cited with gusto by traitorous diplomats. In reality, it was nothing but the result of conflicting interests between the imperialist powers, none of which had any friendly intentions towards China. Indeed, facts soon proved that they all had evil intentions. Tsarist Russia, France and Germany bragged of their "good offices" in the "return of the Liaotung Peninsula" and demanded rewards. Germany seized Kiaochow Bay, tsarist Russia seized Lushun and Talien, and France forcibly leased Kwangchow Bay. Unwilling to lag behind the others, Britain took the opportunity to force the Ching government to grant it the leasehold of Weihaiwei. The imperialist pirates swooped down on China like vultures on a corpse. They marked off different areas, economically and militarily within their reach, as their respective "sphere of influence", and established themselves as masters. Britain's "sphere of influence" was the Yangtse River valley; that of France, Yunnan, Kwangsi and Kwangtung Provinces, a part of Kwangsi and Kwangtung being, however, under British influence; that of Japan, Fukien Province; that of Germany, Shantung Province; and that of tsarist Russia, the three northeastern provinces. China was on the verge of being partitioned. The United States of America arrived late on the scene, and failed to obtain any special "sphere of influence" in China. It, therefore, put forward the cunning "Open Door" policy by which it hoped to seize even more privileges than all the other imperialist countries. On the one hand it tried to court the Chinese people's favour by posing as a defender of the sovereignty and the territorial integrity of China. On the other hand it demanded an "Open Door" so that it could infiltrate into the other imperialist "spheres of influences" and establish itself throughout China. Its ultimate aim was to convert China into a U.S. colony. As time went on this policy became more and more insidious. After World War I, the United States under the pretext of discussing the "Open Door" policy, convened the Washington Conference which drew up a Nine-Power Treaty[1] with terms very favourable for itself.

After World War II, it pursued its plans a step further, intending to use Chiang Kai-shek as a tool to enable the United States to swallow China at one gulp. The United States worked according to this new colonialist plan in China for fifty years. Then, just before it was fully realized, the Chinese people, under the leadership of the Chinese Communist Party, smashed it to smithereens.

After the Sino-Japanese War of 1894, the bourgeois reform movement, stimulated by the national crisis, made some progress under the leadership of Kang Yu-wei and Liang Chi-chao. The doctrine of reform and modernization spread to all parts of the country. Shanghai, Hunan and Kwangtung became three centres of the reform movement. Szechuan was far away in the southwest but the ideas of reform and modernization were also very popular there.

It was at this time that I first came into contact with "the new learning". My elder brother was very fond of reading, and after the end of the mourning period he went back to Tsunching Academy to study. There was a bookstore in Chengtu which, to meet a growing demand, began to sell many kinds of new books and my brother became one of its best customers. He got heavily into debt because of his book purchases. I was then staying in the countryside and he sent me new books regularly. After reading some written by Kang Yu-wei and Liang Chi-chao, especially those of the latter author, which were written in an outspoken and fluent

---

[1] In November 1921 the United States convened a conference in Washington attended by China, Britain, France, Italy, Belgium, Holland, Portugal, Japan and the United States itself, nine countries in all. This was a conference at which the United States and Japan struggled for supremacy in the Far East. On February 6, 1922, a Nine-Power Treaty was concluded in accordance with the United States' proposal of equal opportunity for all countries in China and the "Open Door" policy. The aim of the Nine-Power Treaty was to make possible the joint control of China by the imperialist powers and, as a matter of fact, to pave the way for the United States' monopoly of all China, in order to defeat Japan's plan of swallowing up China alone.

style, I immediately became their follower and was determined to be a protagonist of political reform. My interest in the "eight-legged" essays[1] and competitive examinations quickly dwindled.

After a certain period of publicity and struggle, in January 1898, Kang Yu-wei presented a petition to the emperor, for "overall planning" in which he put forward a systematic programme of reform. He demanded that the emperor solemnly inform the ministers of the adoption of a new national policy, that the government set up an office for receiving petitions and thus enable the people to express their views. There should also be a bureau of institutions to introduce new practices into the government and bureaux of civil administration in the provinces to carry out local autonomy. In other words, he wanted the bourgeoisie to take part in the government and to make China adopt the system of constitutional monarchy, jointly controlled by the landlords and the bourgeoisie. On June 11 of the same year Emperor Kuang Hsu issued an edict on national policy and expressed his determination to carry out political reform. Then the "One-Hundred-Day Reform" began and in rapid succession Emperor Kuang Hsu issued a series of edicts, intended to carry out measures of bourgeois reform from the top. Roughly speaking these measures were as follows: 1) the establishment of modern schools, first of all the Metropolitan College (predecessor of Peking University); 2) the abolition of the competitive examination system and the adoption of a method for the recruitment of new people to official posts; 3) the granting of freedom of speech to the people and encouraging them to make petitions; 4) the

---

[1] The "eight-legged" essay, a special form of essay prescribed by the system of competitive examinations under China's feudalist dynasties from the 15th to 19th centuries, was a juggling with words, utterly void of content and concerned only with form. Every paragraph was written to a rigid pattern and even the number of words was prescribed; the writer spun out the essay by ringing the changes on the words in the theme.

development of industry and the protection and encouragement of agricultural, industrial and commercial enterprises; 5) the abolition of redundant government offices and the reorganization of the existing degenerate armed forces. Owing to the fact that Kuang Hsu was an emperor in name only, and that all power was controlled by the conservative diehards, including the Empress Dowager and her henchman Jung Lu, these measures were not earnestly carried out. Later it became increasingly evident that the measures of political reform were not in accord with the immediate interests of these obstinate conservatives. The abolition of redundant government offices, for instance, meant that many of them would be deprived of their jobs. That being so, they tried not only to wipe out the reformers but to depose the emperor. In their secret plotting they worked out a plan to get Emperor Kuang Hsu and the Empress Dowager to go to Tientsin in October under the guise of reviewing the troops. They would then take the opportunity to stage a coup d'etat. Emperor Kuang Hsu sensed danger and secretly wrote to Kang Yu-wei and asked for help. But what could Kang Yu-wei and his colleagues do? Kang Yu-wei was at most an adviser to the emperor, while Liang Chi-chao was only in charge of matters concerning translation. The four "Little Councillors"[1] were nothing more than four unimportant secretaries. They had neither power nor troops, and could not possibly perform the great task of saving the emperor from danger. Finally they had to ask Yuan Shih-kai, who had troops under his command, for help. He was a shameless crook and immediately betrayed them to the Empress Dowager's right-hand man, Jung Lu. On September 21 the Empress Dowager imprisoned Emperor Kuang Hsu and took over the reins of government herself. Kang Yu-wei and Liang Chi-chao were forced to flee the country. Tan Sze-tung, Yang Jui, Liu Kuang-ti, Lin Hsu,

---

[1] Tan Sze-tung, Yang Jui, Liu Kuang-ti and Lin Hsu were officials who worked in the office of the Grand Council and were known as "Little Councillors".

Yang Shen-hsiu and Kang Kuang-jen, who were known as the "Six Gentlemen", were arrested and executed. This is what the historians call the "Coup d'etat of 1898". Thus the reform movement which lasted for 103 days ended in complete failure.

The failure of the "One-Hundred-Day Reform" proved that in China the reformist path was a blind alley. Many intellectuals therefore took the path of bourgeois revolution. Yet this reform was not without its positive significance in the modern history of China. Although the measures promulgated by the government during the reform of 1898 were insignificant, at the time they did cause a great stir in the country. I had personal experience of this and my impressions are still very clear. I was then studying in the Hsuchuan Academy of Tsekung, southern Szechuan. Owing to my great zeal in propagating the idea of reform and modernization I was nicknamed a "Specialist in Current Affairs". When the edicts proclaiming reforms came one after another I and the other supporters of reform were frantic with joy. We were particularly inspired by the edicts of Emperor Kuang Hsu in which he repeatedly censured the conservatives for obstructing the people when they wished to make petitions. It gave us prestige and silenced the conservatives in the academy who opposed reform. Looking back now I can see that our belief in Emperor Kuang Hsu was very childish, but at that time, we were considered to be most progressive in our ideas, especially in my home district. As we continued to obtain the upper hand in the academy, progressive thought was on the increase there. Unfortunately, this favourable situation did not last long, because the coup d'etat soon followed and the "Six Gentlemen" were murdered. Then the conservatives in the academy launched an immediate counter-offensive against us. They tried to ridicule us, saying, "We told you reform was wrong and that it might cost you your head if you believed in it."

We were not daunted, and cited Tan Sze-tung's heroism as an answer. Before Tan's arrest a certain Japanese national advised him to flee. He refused to do so and said courageously, "In other countries reform has usually been carried out with bloodshed. I have not yet heard of any bloodshed during the recent reform movement and this is the reason why China has not become strong. If there is going to be bloodshed in China let me be the first of the martyrs." The spirit of Tan Sze-tung gave us encouragement and enabled us to stand up boldly to the conservatives. The conservative forces, however, were deep-rooted in China. For thousands of years feudal conventions had fettered the people's ideas and stifled their thoughts. The failure of the reform movement encouraged the obstinate conservatives to become more reckless than ever. All the measures taken during the period of reform were repealed and even minor reforms were rejected. An instance of this was the footbinding of my niece. A "Natural Feet" Association had already been formed in Shanghai. Both my elder brother and I were strongly opposed to footbinding and my eldest brother also sympathized with us. After the failure of the reform movement, my sister-in-law succumbed to the influence of the conservatives, and stubbornly refused to listen to our advice and had her daughter's feet bound. Alas! How could reforms be carried out in the country when even the ways of life in our own home could not be changed? How my heart ached when I thought of this! The instance cited was not merely a matter of our family affairs or simply a matter concerning one girl's feet. It was really part of the serious struggle between the new and the old. As the relative strength of the new and the old stood at the time it was unimaginable that a woman like my sister-in-law would approve of a girl growing up with natural feet. But such ideas were susceptible to change as society progressed. In 1903, when I was in Japan, my own daughter reached the age of footbinding. My wife wrote to tell me that she was going to bind the girl's feet. I wrote back at once expressing strong opposition to this, and my daughter's feet, which had just been bound, were unbound. She became the first woman in my home district to have unbound feet. The action I took was ridiculed at first by relatives and friends, but later people gradually followed my example. This shows that in order to change people's customs and habits there must be objective social conditions which admit of such a change and there must also be people who have the courage to take the lead in making the change and bravely struggle against tradition. The lack of either one of these two factors would have made the attempt impossible.

3. THE UPRISING LED BY YU TUNG-CHEN AND THE YI HO TUAN MOVEMENT

After the failure of the Reform Movement in 1898 the Yi Ho Tuan Movement soon appeared on the scene. This proved to be the greatest peasant revolutionary movement since the failure of the Taiping Revolution. It was directed mainly against the imperialists, especially those who carried out aggressive activities under the cloak of religion. The Chinese people did not oppose religion as such. They merely opposed those who used the name of God to cover up their own evil-doing and misdeeds. During the 19th century, when the capitalist-imperialist powers were waging aggression against China, they frequently used missionaries as their vanguard and the churches as their strongholds. As the imperialists gained strength in China, the criminal activities of lawless foreign missionaries became more and more flagrant. Many Chinese Christians also relied on the power of the foreign missionaries to bully their own people. Thus the Christian churches became more powerful than the Chinese government and any lawsuit involving a dispute with the Christians was invariably considered a hopeless case. The foreign missionaries went in and out of the government offices freely. The shameless Ching officials became obsequious as soon as they saw missionaries and looked upon them as their superiors.

The churches often became big landlords and money-lenders. They exploited the peasants by charging even higher rent and usurious interest than the feudal landlords of China. For all these reasons the Chinese people, especially the peasants, bitterly hated the aggressive activities of the foreign Christian churches. Their anti-imperialist struggle was therefore often carried out in the form of an anti-church struggle. "Church lawsuits", that is, lawsuits between the people and the church became more and more frequent all over China after the sixties. These lawsuits were in reality a form of struggle against the foreign aggressors, operating under the guise of the Christian church. After the ruthless suppression in Tientsin in 1870, this struggle ebbed temporarily. But in the nineties it became vigorous again. The national crisis, which became increasingly acute after the Sino-Japanese War of 1894, gave further impetus to the development of this struggle against imperialism.

The Szechuan people's struggle against the activities of the imperialist aggressors in the church had a long history. In 1863 the people of Chungking were the first to launch an anti-church struggle, known as the first "Church Lawsuit of Chungking". In 1868 there was the famous "Church Lawsuit of Yuyang". The scale of this struggle, which was carried on by the people of Yuyang against the aggressive force in the church, can be judged from the fact that more than 1,000 people were killed or wounded during its course. After 1890 an uprising led by Yu Tung-chen broke out. Yu Tung-chen was a poor peasant from Tatsu County, Szechuan. As a young man he was physically stronger than most people, and being fond of taking up the cudgels against injustices, he was nicknamed "Hot-Headed Yu". At a religious fair held in August 1890, when public indignation was aroused by the unreasonable seizing of some people by church authorities, Yu led the people in an uprising. Later he was caught by government troops and imprisoned. The people who took part in the uprising, however, broke into the Jungchang County prison and released him. They also took this opportunity to seize a French missionary. Then the uprising spread wider. The people not only repeatedly defeated encircling troops of the Ching government but also frustrated the enemy's scheme for luring them into surrender. The insurgents were welcomed everywhere. The influence of the uprising spread to dozens of counties in southeastern Szechuan and the border areas of Hupeh. But owing to the lack of correct ideological guidance, the leaders of the uprising, originally leaders of the Society of Brothers, gradually became corrupt. Those who came from landlord families were not the only ones to show themselves in their true colours; Yu Tung-chen, originally a poor peasant, also became corrupt. The leaders became alienated from the peasant masses and handicraftsmen, lost support and at the beginning of 1899 the insurgent army was defeated by the reactionary Ching troops and Yu Tung-chen was taken captive.

After the Sino-Japanese War in 1894, the people's anti-imperialist struggle in Hupeh, Hunan, Kwangtung, Kwangsi, Shantung and Kiangsu, like that in Szechuan, daily increased in vigour. It was precisely on the basis of the nation-wide anti-imperialist struggle that the Yi Ho Tuan (Society of Righteousness and Harmony) Movement came into being. Originally known as the Yi Ho Chuan (Righteous and Harmonious Fists) it was a secret society organized by the people and strongly coloured by religious superstition. The movement started in Shantung because Germany's aggression in that province was particularly atrocious, and, in addition, Shantung suffered repeatedly from floods, drought and famine during the period 1898-1900. Its leader was Chu Hung-teng. His aim was "to overthrow the Ching and restore the Ming" as well as "to oppose the foreigners and exterminate the church". Yu Hsien, the governor of Shantung, was a great butcher. Once, when he was the prefect of Tsaochow, he massacred more than 2,000 members of the Big

Sword Society.[1] He did not succeed, however, in killing all the members of the Big Sword Society, and narrowly escaped being killed by them himself. When the Yi Ho Chuan first arose he tried hard to suppress it but, failing in this, he then tried to make use of it. Later the Ching rulers changed the name Yi Ho Chuan into Yi Ho Tuan and reorganized it into a militia under government control. They also changed the society's principle of "fighting against the Ching and exterminating the foreigners" into "supporting the Ching and exterminating the foreigners", hoping thereby to change the target of the people's revolutionary struggle by taking advantage of their hatred towards the foreigners. The Chinese people's hatred of foreigners was very widespread at the time, but it was a blanket hatred, making no distinction between good and bad. The people only thought that all would be well in China if the foreigners were driven out. This was the view of the Empress Dowager, of many of the officials in the government and of the people. The Empress Dowager and government officials dared not come out in the open but wanted to use the people as their tools against the foreigners. It is easy to understand how the Yi Ho Tuan did, in fact, become their tool. The imperialists were angry with Yu Hsien for making use of the Yi Ho Tuan, and they compelled the Ching government to remove him from office. Complying with the dictates of the imperialists the Ching government transferred Yu Hsien to Shansi and appointed Yuan Shih-kai as his successor. The ruthless suppression carried out by Yuan Shih-kai inflicted a setback on the Yi Ho Tuan in Shantung and Chu Hung-teng, its leader, was captured and killed. By 1900 the influence of the society had spread to Hopei and soon afterwards branches were established in Tientsin, Paoting and even in the vicinity of Peking. In these places, which were

---

[1] The Big Sword Society was a secret society organized by the people of northern China. It was an armed force with which the peasants fought against the landlords. The members of the society carried big swords, hence its name.

centres of reactionary rule, members of the Yi Ho Tuan attacked missionaries and set fire to their churches. Neither the Ching government nor the imperialists knew what to do. Under such conditions the cunning Empress Dowager accepted Yu Hsien's advice. She declared war on the foreign powers but ordered the Yi Ho Tuan, whose members were armed only with spears and lances, to fight the imperialist troops who possessed both rifles and cannons. She also sent a secret apology to the imperialists and informed them that the declaration of war was made under pressure from the "bandits". Under the pretext of protecting the embassies and suppressing the "bandits" on behalf of the Ching government, Britain, the United States, Germany, France, tsarist Russia, Japan, Italy and Austria organized an allied army and attempted to suppress the Yi Ho Tuan. The Yi Ho Tuan stubbornly resisted the offensives of the imperialists. Serious blows were dealt to the aggressors at Tientsin, Yangtsun, Langfang, and Changchiakou. Despite its modern army of more than 40,000 men after several months of fighting, the imperialists were only able to take several transport lines from Shanhaikuan in the east to Changchiakou in the west and Chengting in the south. Although they reached the border of Shansi they did not dare to go into the Taihang Mountains, as they were afraid of the influence and power of the Yi Ho Tuan. When the imperialist troops arrived in Peking the cowardly Empress Dowager hastily fled to Sian and appointed the rank traitor Li Hung-chang as her plenipotentiary representative, to sue for peace. Thus the imperialists and all the feudal forces in China joined hands again and under their joint attack the Yi Ho Tuan was finally defeated. Li Hung-chang, an out-and-out comprador-henchman for the foreigners, was always against the Yi Ho Tuan and against its being used as a tool to oppose his masters, the foreign powers, as was advocated by the Empress Dowager and Yu Hsien. When the Yi Ho Tuan Movement was in full swing in the north, influential provincial governors, like Liu Kun-yi, Chang Chih-tung, Li Hung-chang and Yuan

Shih-kai, worked hand in glove with the imperialists, and refused to carry out the Ching government's order to declare war on the imperialist powers. To protect themselves they adopted a policy of "neutrality" in Shantung and the provinces in the southeast. The purpose of the eight imperialist powers in organizing the allied army was to realize their long-cherished plan of partitioning China. The strong resistance offered by the Yi Ho Tuan made them realize that it was absolutely impossible for them to rule the country directly. They then concluded that the partitioning of China was by no means feasible[1] and that the best thing for them to do was to rule China through the Chinese.[2] At the time there were many contradictions within the ranks of the imperialist powers. In the scramble for privileges the various foreign powers were more than once on the verge of an armed conflict between themselves during the period when they occupied Peking. Finally, however, they all arrived at the same conclusion that it was better for China to remain a nominally independent country and for the Ching government to rule in their interest. It was under such conditions that Li Hung-chang and others negotiated with the imperialists and signed the traitorous International Protocol in September 1901. This protocol, which was very harsh in its terms, contained the following stipulations: the Ching government was to severely punish those officials who were openly "anti-foreign", and to strictly prohibit "anti-foreign" activities among the people; the imperialist powers were to be allowed to station troops in important cities and towns between Peking, Tientsin and Shan-haikuan; the Ching government was to pay the powers 450 million taels as "indemnities", and the customs revenues and the revenues from the salt tax were assigned as security for the payment.

---

[1] Refers to a statement made by Alfred von Waldersee, commander of the eight powers' allied army.

[2] Refers to a statement made by W.A.P. Martin, an American missionary.

Kang Yu-wei in 1898

Liang Chi-chao in 1898

The Yi Ho Tuan fighting a battle

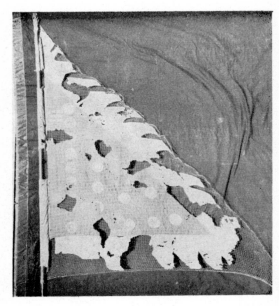

Flag of the Yi Ho Tuan

The invasion of Peking by the eight powers' allied army and the signing of the Protocol of 1901 made all patriotic Chinese feel humiliated and angry. I remember that a certain newspaper carried a poem which contained these two lines:

It is still the same road leading to Shanhaikuan,
But, alas, flags of many colours are fluttering
everywhere.

It made my blood boil when I read them. The influence of the Yi Ho Tuan spread to my home district, where the Red Lantern Sect, a secret society similar to the Yi Ho Tuan, became quite active. One of my nephews joined the sect. Every day, he and his companions drilled with swords and spears. They chanted something along these lines, "A piece of red silk is waved, the heavenly soldiers are moving and the gods are coming down to the mundane world." At that time I was already under the influence of the "new learning" and had a smattering of scientific knowledge. I thought it was absurd to believe in such feudal superstitions but I had a great respect for the revolutionary spirit of the Red Lantern Sect in its attacks on the churches and opposition to foreign aggressors. Because of this contradiction in my outlook and also inasmuch as I was a member of the literati, the first of the four classes of people,[1] I adopted an indifferent, "neutral" attitude towards this movement. I only saw the backward side of the Yi Ho Tuan but I did not know how this backwardness originated nor did I know how to overcome it. Still less was I aware of the fact that although the Yi Ho Tuan was backward in form, the core of the righteous struggle of the peasant masses was an extremely strong revolutionary force. To fully understand this truth it is necessary to study Marxism and of course, under the conditions of that time, I was unable to understand the deep significance of the Yi Ho Tuan Movement. It should be noted, however, that both the

---

[1] Scholars, farmers, artisans and merchants.

uprising led by Yu Tung-chen and the Yi Ho Tuan Movement had a good influence upon the revolutionary activities which I was later to carry out. It was partly due to this influence that shortly before the Revolution of 1911 I was actively engaged in the work of recruiting the aid of various secret societies and organizing the Society for Mutual Progress. This influence was also responsible for the considerable attention I paid to the study of the peasants' land problem during the First and Second Revolutionary Civil Wars.[1] The experiences gained in long years of revolutionary struggle enabled me to gradually understand that a revolutionary's attitude towards the revolutionary movement of the broad masses (although it may appear extremely simple or even backward) must be as Mao Tse-tung has taught us: We should not obstruct it; nor should we stand aside gesticulating at it and criticizing it; it is only by throwing ourselves into the mighty current of mass struggle with full enthusiasm, by courageously guiding the masses forward with a correct theory, that we can lead the revolutionary struggle to success. That is the only correct attitude that a revolutionary can take.

4. SAILING FOR JAPAN

After the failure of the Reform Movement in 1898 my interest in the "new learning" did not diminish; on the contrary it grew steadily. In addition to reading new periodicals I began to study such books as T. H. Huxley's *Evolution and*

---

[1] The First Revolutionary Civil War was an anti-imperialist and anti-feudal revolutionary struggle carried out jointly by the Chinese Communist Party and the Kuomintang from 1924 to 1927, its main task being to launch the Northern Expedition against the northern warlords. This revolution failed because it was betrayed by the reactionary Kuomintang group led by Chiang Kai-shek. The Second Revolutionary Civil War began in 1927 and lasted until 1937. It was a revolutionary struggle of the people led by the Chinese Communist Party for the creation and development of Red political power.

Ethics. Many intellectuals at that time were stimulated by the theories of "natural selection" and "survival of the fittest" expounded in this book. They seemed to sound a warning to us to guard against the danger of national destruction and to struggle for survival. *Evolution and Ethics* explains social phenomena by the theory of evolution as found in nature. That is, of course, wrong. Huxley's theory was later developed and used by the imperialists as a basis for their aggressive actions against the smaller and weaker nations. During the early years of the 20th century, however, *Evolution and Ethics* did play a positive role in China. Students of history must not ignore the fact that the same thought may have different effects under different historical conditions.

From 1900 to 1901 I was a tutor to the children of a big landlord living in the county town. In 1902 I went to Weiyuan to continue my studies. By this time the periodicals *New People's Journal* and *New Novels* had appeared and I was very fond of reading them. It was the custom for students to take the competitive examinations, and although I was no longer interested in them, nevertheless, I took them, too. Fortunately the method of examination had changed. In 1901 the stereotyped "eight-legged" essay had been abolished and the expository style was adopted instead. I made full use of my knowledge of the "new learning" when writing essays for the examinations. Three examinations were necessary to obtain the degree of licentiate — the county and prefectural examinations and one given by the commissioner of studies. There were five tests each in the county and prefectural examinations which lasted for about two weeks; it was quite an ordeal. I took the examinations for the licentiate degree in 1902, and did admirably well in the county and prefectural examinations. In one of the tests in the prefectural examination I was first on the list and the official who read my essay wrote a lengthy laudatory comment on it. I was then about to take the examination given by the commissioner of studies. As I had been second in the last test at the prefectural examination, my paper was to be read by the commissioner of studies.[1] But the essay I wrote during the commissioner's examination was too long and as I did not finish writing it on time, I failed. I did not feel badly about my failure though my relatives and friends were sorry for me. I now look upon it as my good fortune to have failed in that examination because it launched me on to the path of revolution. I had a good friend whose name was Chou Hsien-teng who was very interested in the "new learning" and was one of the progressives of the time. He had been a licentiate, and after passing the provincial examination in 1903, he received a provincial graduate degree. Then he attended China's last metropolitan examination held in Kaifeng. Although he did not pass this examination, he was sent together with many provincial graduates and palace graduates to study in Japan. It was precisely because he was successful in his literary career and blindly followed the reformist doctrine of Kang Yu-wei and Liang Chi-chao that gradually he became reactionary and opposed the revolution.

Failure in the examination made me all the more eager to seek new knowledge. In December 1902 I went to Luchow and enrolled in the Chingwei School there. The Chingwei was supposed to be a school of the "new learning" but in reality it was a school of the "old learning". It even used the feudal classic *Book of Ritual* for a course of study and made quite a fuss about the teaching of feudal etiquette. It also gave a course in English but this was only intended as window-dressing. Only six letters of the alphabet were taught in a week and this slow method of study was exasperating. Unable to stand this, I stayed at the school for two weeks, and left for home in a temper. After that I no longer thought of attending any "modern school" in Szechuan again.

Towards the end of 1902, when I was feeling very depressed about my future, my elder brother returned from Chengtu.

---

[1] In the examination given by the commissioner of studies the papers of the first ten successful examinees in the last test at the prefectural examination were invariably read by the commissioner himself.

He and Huang Chih, one of his schoolmates in the Tsunching Academy, had already made the necessary arrangements to go to Japan to study. I was extremely excited, when I heard that there was an opportunity to study abroad. I decided to go with them. At that time I had been married for six years and had a four-year-old daughter and a two-year-old son. My wife and children were dear to me and I hated to part with them, but with thoughts of how my studies could help the motherland and my own future, I put personal feelings aside. My eldest brother did everything possible to find money for our expenses, even selling some of our farmland. Finally he managed to get together about 200 taels of silver. This was not enough for our expenses but we were not discouraged. It was decided that I should first go to Shanghai with my elder brother and wait there for a chance to go to Japan.

On February 9, 1903, while people were happily celebrating the Spring Festival with drums and gongs, a group of nine of us quietly left our home county and set out by boat. Like Hsuan Tsang[1] of old, who undertook the long journey away from home in quest of sacred scriptures, we were motivated by a noble aim and strong determination. Passing Chungking we arrived at Hsinglungtan where a landslide had just occurred and sailing was very dangerous, but we were undaunted. Full of inspiration and courage we were not afraid of any danger. Sailing on smoothly we arrived at Ichang in eastern Hupeh Province. We were enchanted by the beauty of our motherland as we passed through the Three Gorges of the Yangtse and became quite poetic. Using "Thoughts on My Way to Japan" as a theme we began to compose poems in order to express our feelings. I remember that my poem contained these two lines:

Say not that all are backward in the East;
Standing up in Asia are the people of the yellow race.

---

[1] Hsuan Tsang (602-664) was a famous Buddhist monk of the Tang Dynasty. He left China for India in A.D. 629 and returned in 645.

At that time I did not know how to look at things from the viewpoint of class analysis. Moreover, under the influence of Kang Yu-wei and Liang Chi-chao, I still believed that China should follow Japan's example and imitate Emperor Mutsu-hito's reforms. I had, however, little respect for the Western imperialist countries and felt highly confident about the future of China.

In Shanghai I learned that not much money was needed to study in Japan. I changed my original plan and decided to go to Japan with my brother immediately. We stayed about a fortnight in Shanghai before we sailed. During that short stay I had some extremely valuable experiences. Previously I knew only the reformist doctrine of Kang Yu-wei and Liang Chi-chao, but in Shanghai I began to hear about the theory of bourgeois revolution as advocated by Dr. Sun Yat-sen, Chang Tai-yen and others. Although I only understood a little of it, that was enough to show me that it was a much more convincing theory and my faith in Kang Yu-wei and Liang Chi-chao was severely shaken.

On my way from Shanghai to Japan I made the acquaintance of a woman named Lin Tsung-su. Coming from the hinterland of Szechuan I was surprised to see a woman going abroad for her education. Listening to her conversation, which was mostly about the theory of revolution, I regarded her with great respect. I began to feel the pulse of the times and the tide of revolution began to break down my reformist ideas.

We arrived in Tokyo in March 1903. The tide of revolution was again rising in China and the Chinese students in Japan, co-ordinating with the people in China, were engaged in a struggle against tsarist Russia's occupation of China's northeastern territory. This was the famous Resist-Russia Movement which I joined immediately after my arrival in Tokyo. My life had entered a new phase.

5. THE RESIST-RUSSIA MOVEMENT OF 1903

In 1900 when the eight powers' allied army occupied Peking, tsarist Russia took the opportunity to occupy the three northeastern provinces of China. At the beginning of 1903 she refused to evacuate them according to previous agreement. This aroused the indignation of Chinese people everywhere and the Resist-Russia Movement began. Inside the country, the students of the Metropolitan College held rallies and signed petitions. The people from all walks of life in Shanghai held a mammoth resist-Russia meeting and sent a circular telegram to the people of the whole country calling on them to wage a struggle. Outside the country, the most vigorous Resist-Russia Movement was amongst the Chinese students in Japan. As already mentioned, the movement had already been fully launched before I arrived. I remember that at a students' meeting in the Kinki Hostel great indignation was expressed and a resolution was unanimously passed to organize a students' resist-Russia association. It was agreed to send Tang Erh-ho and Niu Yung-chien back to China with a petition demanding that Yuan Shih-kai resist Russia with armed forces. It may be noted, in passing, that both Tang and Niu later became bureaucrat-politicians who cringed before the warlords. Tang sank so low as to even become a traitor to China. Yuan Shih-kai had just succeeded to Li Hung-chang's post and, acting in accordance with the wish of the reactionary Empress Dowager, was trying to appease Russia in every way. To ask him for help was like asking a tiger for its skin. This shows how naive the students were. As might be expected Yuan Shih-kai refused to see Tang Erh-ho and Niu Yung-chien. This made the students so angry that they organized the Resist-Russia Volunteers. Later the volunteers were reorganized into the Society for Military Education. Lan Tien-wei and Fang Sheng-tao, cadets of the Military Academy in Japan, were asked to be the instructors. The students wanted to learn something of practical value and hoped that they would later serve their country on the battlefield. The embassy of the Ching government tried its utmost to sabotage the Students' Resist-Russia Movement. It said that the students were "in reality working for the revolution under the pretext of resisting Russia" and proposed that the movement be suppressed. Lan Tien-wei and Fang Sheng-tao, both government-supported students, were therefore punished. The movement lasted for a very long time and in February 1904 when the Russo-Japanese War[1] began the students out of hatred for tsarist Russia, even sympathized with Japan. When they heard that Japan had won a victory they were exultant. Looking backwards this seems exceedingly childish. Both Japan and tsarist Russia were imperialist countries and enemies of China. Why then should we look on them differently? It was precisely because Japan took advantage of the Chinese people's hatred of tsarist Russia that it was able to gain many victories in northeastern China very speedily. It was also because of the people's opposition both inside and outside the country that tsarist Russia was badly beaten and had to admit its defeat by a country much smaller and more backward than itself. From this we can see that the will of the people is something which cannot be ignored. I joined the Students' Resist-Russia Association not because I was politically conscious, but because I saw that many people were doing so and I went along with the current. Later I joined the Society for Military Education in the same way. Although I did not join the movement with a clear understanding of its significance the movement nevertheless made

---

[1] This was the imperialist war fought between Japan and tsarist Russia in 1904-05 to grab China's Northeast and Korea. As the war was fought mainly in the area of Fengtien (now Shenyang) and Liaoyang and around the port of Lushun in China's Northeast, it caused enormous losses to the Chinese people. As a result of the war tsarist Russia was defeated and supplanted by Japanese imperialism in the dominant role in China's Northeast. Under the Treaty of Portsmouth concluded at the end of this war tsarist Russia also recognized Japan's exclusive control over Korea.

a big change in my life and pushed me into the rapid current of revolution. At the Kinki meeting in Tokyo, when we were asked to sign our names and join the Students' Resist-Russia Association my brother and I signed without the slightest hesitation. Our old friend Huang Chih and his followers not only refused to sign their own names but looked at our signatures with evident disapproval. Huang Chih was older than my brother and had a higher social position, being a senior licentiate by the competitive examination of 1902. We had gone to Japan under his guidance and he was regarded as our patron. How could this patron, a follower of Kang Yu-wei and Liang Chi-chao, who later became a constitutional monarchist and stood only for "civilized reform", allow his proteges to join a radical revolutionary movement? But we did join it. Unable to stop us from joining he wrote a letter home saying that we had refused to listen to his advice and had joined the revolution. This caused a big disturbance at home and alarmed some of our relatives and friends. They said that we would never be able to return home again, even if we were fortunate enough to save our own lives. Fortunately my eldest brother and my wife knew that my elder brother and I were honest men and would never do anything detrimental to our nation or people, so they were not alarmed. When my eldest brother wrote us about the letter, I was very angry. That a man like Huang Chih should have done such a thing was beyond my comprehension. Looking back I now see there was nothing strange about what he did, however dishonourable it might appear to be, because he followed a different political line from ours. As a result I was forced to become a revolutionary no matter whether I wanted to or not. "Since I can't go home again," I thought, "I might as well devote my whole life to the revolution."

A deeper analysis shows that I took the path of revolution mainly because I was greatly influenced by current progressive ideas. Around the time of the Reform Movement of 1898, especially just before it, the reformist ideas propagated by

Kang Yu-wei and Liang Chi-chao were very popular and did play a positive role. But, after the failure of the Yi Ho Tuan Movement and the uprising led by Tang Tsai-chang,[1] especially the latter, the influence of Kang Yu-wei and Liang Chi-chao's ideas gradually declined with the fall of their political prestige. Originally many political groups ranging from the Society for the Revival of China to the Defend-the-Emperor Society had all taken part in Tang Tsai-chang's Independent Army uprising. After its failure the differences between the revolutionaries and reformers became more and more marked. Meanwhile, owing to his embezzlement of military funds subscribed for the uprising, Kang Yu-wei was attacked by the revolutionaries and became notorious. subsequently, the idea of national revolution promulgated by Chang Tai-yen and other revolutionaries, which aimed at the overthrow of the Manchu rule and the restoration of China to the Hans, gradually became the main current of thought at that time. On April 26, 1902, the anniversary of the death of the last emperor of the Ming Dynasty, Chang Tai-yen and others held a meeting to commemorate the 242nd anniversary of national subjugation to show their determined opposition to the reactionary rule of the Ching government. The periodical *Kiangsu News* then appeared, followed by the *Chekiang Tide, Kiangsu,* etc., all of which were devoted to the spread of revolutionary ideas. In the summer of 1903 Tsou Jung published a pamphlet, *The Revolutionary Army,* which shed new light on the principle of revolution. In this pamphlet

[1] In August 1900, Tang Tsai-chang and other members of the Defend-the-Emperor Society, which was founded by Kang Yu-wei and Liang Chi-chao, organized an Independent Army in Hankow and other places along the middle reaches of the Yangtse River and, under the slogan of opposing the Empress Dowager and supporting Emperor Kuang Hsu, they launched an armed uprising which, however, soon failed. From its political aim it can be seen that it was a continuation of the Reform Movement after the coup d'etat of 1898. Tang Tsai-chang and his group once had connections with the revolutionary Society for the Revival of China. Knowing their political aim the revolutionaries were greatly dissatisfied with them and a breach soon followed.

Tsou Jung praised revolution with great zeal. Written in a clear and penetrating style, it was widely read and played a great agitational role among the people. Owing to historical and class limitations of that period the revolutionary idea which he advocated was mainly bourgeois nationalism with a slight tinge of bourgeois democracy. Quite a few passages in his pamphlet were tainted by biased ideas and narrow-mindedness. Looking at it now, the pamphlet is obviously outdated, but in Tsou Jung's time its publication had considerable influence which helped to change people's idea of bourgeois reformism to that of bourgeois revolution. Its historical importance therefore must not be ignored. At about the same time, having paid tribute to *The Revolutionary Army* in the *Kiangsu News,* Chang Tai-yen wrote an article, "Kang Yu-wei's Theory of Revolution Refuted", in which he bluntly called Emperor Kuang Hsu, the idol of Kang Yu-wei and Liang Chi-chao, "a clown". This was a blow to the reformers and stimulated revolutionary thought. After that, the influence of the reformers gradually declined while that of the revolutionaries became stronger and stronger. I had already had my first contact with revolutionary thought on my way to Japan, and after my arrival there I came more and more under the influence of revolutionary ideas and took part in the Students' Resist-Russia Movement. Thus I gradually shed my reformist ideas. Therefore, when I heard Huang Chih had told my family that I supported the revolution I was not upset; on the contrary, I was even more determined to work for the revolution. I cut off my queue[1] in a fit of anger to show that I would never retract. In those days, although a large number of Chinese students in Japan cut off their queues many still retained them. Many Chinese stu-

---

[1] It was a custom of the Manchus for men to wear queues. The Ching government forced the Han people to accept this custom, which was therefore regarded by the Hans as a sign of subjugation. The revolutionaries cut their queues to show their determination to overthrow the Manchu rule.

dents attending the Military Academy, for instance, still wore queues but concealed them under their caps. After having experienced these changes and read Tsou Jung's *The Revolutionary Army* and other writings I decided to abandon reformist ideas.

6. IN THE SEIJO SCHOOL

When we arrived in Japan there were not many Chinese students there, the total number being only about a thousand. The number of Szechuan students was much smaller. Only about thirty were present at the welcome party given us by the Szechuan students. We all felt it necessary to ask the people of our home province to send more students to study abroad and we decided to write and circulate an essay entitled "On the Advantage of Sending Students to Study Abroad". We sent a petition to the provincial authorities of Szechuan asking them to send one or two government-supported students from each county to study in the short-term normal schools of Japan so that they would be able to establish modern schools when they returned. We also proposed that the county governments subsidize the self-supporting students. These two documents played a great role in helping the Szechuan people to realize the importance of sending students to study in Japan. Thus, beginning from 1904, the number of Szechuan students studying in Japan rapidly increased and once reached the record number of three thousand. Our plan to promote the sending of students to study abroad was adopted in many other provinces, especially after 1904 when the competitive examination system had been abolished and, following the opening of modern schools, teachers were urgently needed in all parts of China. Consequently, students from counties in various provinces were sent to study in the Japanese short-term normal schools. The number of Chinese students in Japan increased so rapidly that by 1905 it exceeded 10,000.

On our arrival in Japan my brother and I had to decide which school we should enter. This was an important question. My elder brother decided on the Kobun Normal School. I wanted to study for a longer time and planned to begin in secondary school and then go to college to study science and engineering. At that time there were two Szechuan students studying these subjects in the Seijo School. They said to me, "If you want to study science and engineering you must have a good foundation," and advised me not to enter a private school because many were badly run and it would be a waste of time. They said that I would be very lucky if I got into the Seijo. Previously the Seijo had been a preparatory school for the Military Academy and only admitted a small number of students who wished to study the arts. But now as a juvenile military school had been established as the preparatory school for the academy, the Seijo was to become a five-year secondary school and would not enrol Chinese students. Considering the Seijo was strict in discipline and had good teachers, the two Szechuan students thought it a great pity that Chinese students could not enrol. I thought so too. Consequently I asked them to have a talk with the principal of the school and request him to continue the two-and-half-year short-term course in arts for the benefit of the Chinese students. The principal agreed but said that there must be a minimum of twenty students before the class could be opened. I tried my utmost to·find twenty students but failed after being several times on the verge of success. Failure, however, did not discourage me, and I finally succeeded in getting more than this required twenty students for the class. The Seijo was really a very good school, and the teachers were very strict with the students. The students boarded at the school and were not allowed to go out except on Sundays and on Wednesday and Saturday afternoons. The teachers were competent. I particularly remember that there was a teacher

63

of mathematics, a research student in a teacher's college, who taught very well. He made me realize that although old teachers with rich experience command respect, young teachers with zeal and knowledge are invaluable in a school. Under his tutorship my mathematics greatly improved and the solutions to problems worked out by myself were almost as correct as those demonstrated in the lectures. Thanks to the strict training provided by the school, the courses which usually took five years were completed in two and half years, and with good results. The admirable teaching method in the Seijo left a deep impression on me and I am sure it conformed with correct educational principles. As an old Chinese saying goes, "If the teacher is not strict it means that he is lazy." The Chinese people have always believed that only strict teachers can produce good pupils. It behoves modern educators to think this over. When this first short-term course at the Seijo proved to be successful students began to stream in. After that several hundred Chinese students attended the Seijo every year and thousands graduated from the school.

The Japanese government established the Shinbu School which only admitted Chinese students preparing for the Military Academy. Only government-supported Chinese students were admitted to the Shinbu School and the Military Academy. The opposition parties in Japan established the private Tohin School for self-supporting Chinese students who wished to study military science. A large number of Chinese students also attended the Hosei University in Tokyo. Practically all the provincial graduates who took the last competitive examination held in Kaifeng in 1904, no matter whether they were successful or not, went to Japan and entered this university. Thus the students were largely youths from high officials' families.

While studying in the Seijo, although school work was heavy, I continued carrying out revolutionary activities. I was the monitor of the first class in the Seijo School and a staff member of the Overseas Chinese Club for Students, responsible for liaison and entertainment. I was busy with a great many social activities both within and without the school.

Most of the money which my brother and I had brought from home was used up by the beginning of 1904. When my brother returned to China, I was left in extremely straitened circumstances. I was frequently in arrears in the payment of my tuition fee and when my schoolmates learned of my plight they wanted to petition the government of my county for a subsidy on my behalf. I had gone to Japan at a comparatively early period. I was the monitor of the first class in the Seijo School and my school work was good. My family was really poor. In such circumstances the county subsidy would have been granted in answer to a petition by my schoolmates. But from early childhood I had been brought up to follow the ancient moral principle, "Don't accept money which you should not accept and don't shun difficult tasks which you should not shun." I resolutely refused to accept my schoolmates' good offices and suggested that another student, needier than I, have the subsidy. In order to ensure that we should have a student of military science in our county I suggested that we petition the county government to subsidize Lo Hou-chang. All agreed to do so and the subsidy was granted. As a result of this my schoolmates understood me better and the relation between us became much closer. When the school authorities saw that I was respected by my schoolmates, they also treated me very kindly, never pressed me for my tuition fee and gave me the usual monthly allowance of pocket money. On my part, I did my best not to postpone the payment of my tuition fee too long. Every time a remittance came from home the first thing I did was to pay the arrears. With the help of my schoolmates and the kindness shown to me by the school authorities I was actually able to finish my studies without interruption. From this it can be seen that if you care for others they will care for you and if you try to harm others you will end by harming yourself. No one will come to a good end by acting contrary to the interest of the masses.

Although the school authorities were very kind to me I never stopped participating in any struggle which I felt should be waged. I remember that on New Year's Day, 1904, when the flags of various countries were hung up in the school the Chinese flag was conspicuous by its absence. The Chinese students were very indignant and I led them in a determined protest. We told the school authorities that unless they hung up the Chinese flag and apologized we would not attend class and would go on a hunger-strike. "We have been so good to you," the school authorities said to me, "why do you lead the students to oppose the school?" "I feel very grateful to the school for its kindness to me," I answered, "but if a matter concerns the honour of my country I must fight with all my might!" Under the impact of the Chinese students' united action the school authorities finally gave in. It had always been the policy of the Japanese imperialists to wheedle and win over the Chinese students by hook or by crook. There were some Chinese students in Japan who were willing to sacrifice principle for profit and who allowed themselves to come under the influence of the Japanese. Some of them later betrayed their country. The test of a person's courage in upholding national honour is whether he can place the interest of his country and people above his own. I have always regarded the interest of the nation as sacred. This was the reason why, as soon as I was confronted with a case in which China was insulted by the Japanese imperialists, I immediately disregarded the previous goodwill I had towards them. After this incident and the 1905 struggle against the Japanese regulation to exercise supervision over Chinese and Korean students studying in Japan, my hatred of Japanese imperialism increased in direct proportion to its intensification of aggression against China. The struggle against Japanese imperialism and for the existence of the Chinese nation thereafter occupied a prominent place in my life.

7.   THE ANTI-U.S. MOVEMENT OF 1905

Although the U.S. imperialists are more cunning and hypocritical than all the other imperialists, nevertheless their aggressive policy is everywhere opposed by its victims.   It took the Chinese people many years to see through the aggressive nature of U.S. imperialism.   As soon as they knew the truth they displayed a giant's strength, kicking it, together with its henchmen, like a heap of rubbish, completely off the Chinese mainland.   At present the people of Asia, Africa and Latin America are all awakening.   The U.S. imperialists will continue to play all kinds of tricks and the struggle of these people will have its ups and downs.   But with the experience of the Chinese people as an example and under the favourable conditions of the present world situation, they will without doubt win their victory, and before an unduly long period of time.   The last and most powerful neo-colonialist country, the imperialist United States, is now rushing to its doom as determined by the immutable laws of history.

Among the Chinese there were certain people who for a long time were deceived by the U.S. imperialists.   This was especially true of those who had connections with the U.S. imperialists and their lackeys.   It was also true of those who were educated in American schools and were influenced by American thought and way of life.   The broad masses of the people, however, especially the toilers who have been directly exploited and bullied by the U.S. imperialists, have always waged an unremitting, patriotic struggle against them.   The anti-U.S., patriotic struggle of the Chinese people has a long history and has enabled them to gain rich experiences.   The 1905 anti-U.S. movement, for instance, was a nation-wide patriotic struggle which wielded a powerful influence and was carried out under extremely complicated conditions.

The anti-U.S., patriotic movement of 1905 was touched off by the people's demand for the termination of the American-Chinese emigration treaty of 1894.   It opposed the discrimination against and persecution of Chinese workers in the United States. Many gold, silver, coal and iron mines as well as many railway lines and municipal works in the western part of the United States were opened and built with the sweat and blood of Chinese workers. Consequently there were a large number of overseas Chinese in that part of America. The China Town of San Francisco, for instance, was almost entirely inhabited by Chinese people. When the American capitalists needed cheap labourers they used all devices, such as lying, enticing and even kidnapping, to get Chinese workers to go to the United States. These poorly paid workers created enormous profits for the American capitalists. This can be clearly seen from the American-Chinese treaty of 1868. In times of economic crisis, the capitalists maligned Chinese workers, saying that they had robbed the American workers of their jobs, thus making the Chinese workers and not themselves the target of the American workers' struggle. They discriminated against Chinese workers to deceive American workers, and deliberately fomented anti-Chinese incidents. It was under such conditions that the American-Chinese emigration treaty of 1894 was signed. After signing this anti-Chinese treaty with the corrupt Ching government the Americans interpreted it as they pleased, using the treaty to intensify their persecution and maltreatment of Chinese workers. At the same time they freely insulted all Chinese nationals who went to the United States. On landing they were invariably shut up in wooden huts where they had to wait like prisoners until they were taken to the authorities for examination. Under the pretext of preventing the spread of diseases, caustic chemicals were often poured over the clothes, luggage and even the bare bodies of Chinese nationals. The beating and insulting of Chinese immigrants and the burning of their houses were common occurrences. This greatly injured the Chinese people's national pride and when the treaty expired in 1904 the people of all social strata in China demanded its abrogation and opposed the signing of a new treaty.

Towards the end of 1904 newspapers and magazines in all parts of the country began to discuss the question of abolishing the American-Chinese immigration treaty. Soon many articles appeared, exposing the U.S. imperialists' maltreatment of Chinese workers. The Chinese people's hatred of U.S. imperialism was steadily intensified. In the spring of 1905 when the people heard that the U.S. imperialists planned to sign a new treaty with the Ching government the anti-U.S. movement began to spread with increasing vigour. In May of that year the Shanghai Chamber of Commerce passed a resolution to the effect that if the U.S. imperialists did not stop maltreating Chinese workers and overseas Chinese within two months it would launch a movement to boycott American goods. Meanwhile an anti-U.S. movement began to unfold in various other places. When the two months' limit expired in July the U.S. imperialists still insisted on signing a new treaty. The Chinese people were indignant and the anti-U.S. movement came to its apex with the boycott of American goods. The movement was unprecedented in scale. With Shanghai as its centre it swept over the whole country and even spread abroad. The U.S. imperialists urged the Ching government to repress the movement. The *Chinese and Foreign Daily,* run by the comprador capitalist Wang Kangnien, whose interest was tied up with U.S. imperialism, tried repeatedly to sabotage the movement. After the bourgeoisie, represented by Tseng Chu, president of the Shanghai Chamber of Commerce, had launched the movement it wavered and then withdrew from it. The broad working masses were undaunted, and persisted in their struggle with the result that the Ching government did not dare to conclude a new treaty with the U.S. imperialists. The Chinese working class, still in its infancy, displayed great activity and perseverance in this struggle. In addition to taking part in the general movement to boycott American goods the transport workers refused to handle American goods, postmen refused to accept mail containing samples of American goods and factory workers refused to use American raw materials. After the bourgeoisie withdrew from the movement, the workers in Shanghai held a meeting in Yuyuan Park at the end of October. Their persistence in the struggle brought a certain amount of success. It should be noted that there were also people among the national bourgeoisie who were comparatively firm in support of the struggle. Yu Chih-mo, president of the Hunan Chamber of Commerce, may be mentioned as a typical example. From this we can see that in semi-colonial and semi-feudal China the working class was the most revolutionary class while the bourgeoisie was extremely weak and showed signs of divergence from the very beginning.

The influence of the anti-U.S., patriotic movement of 1904 extended to other countries. Many of the Chinese students in Japan joined in the movement, those from Szechuan being especially active. The members of the Szechuanese Club, composed largely of students, once held a meeting in Ueno Park in Tokyo for the express purpose of discussing ways and means of boycotting American goods. They passed a resolution pledging themselves to get in touch with the people of Chengtu, Chungking and other places for the purpose of launching a movement in Szechuan to boycott American goods. It was the activities of the Chinese students in Japan that inspired the subsequent launching of such a movement in Chengtu, Chungking and other places. Why were these students so enthusiastic? The reason is simple. Although most of them came from feudal families and had some backward and reactionary ideas they differed from students who came from comprador families. They were untainted by contact with imperialists and were therefore comparatively active in the anti-imperialist, patriotic struggle. Coming from the outlying districts of China they were strongly provincial in outlook and desirous of unity. They liked to discuss current affairs and criticize the things they considered unjust, and were easily involved in all kinds of struggles. The level of their political consciousness rose as a result of their participation in struggle. Many of them joined the Revolutionary League and made considerable contributions to the Revolution of 1911. Their reasons for joining various struggles differed widely. Quite a number of them were really patriotic, but some merely made use of mass movements as a ladder to fame and wealth. There were also those who did it to show off, some just drifted with the current without any particular aim. As for the really patriotic students, the enthusiasm of most of them did not last. They showed the characteristics of the petty-bourgeois intellectuals blowing hot and cold, and were prone to vacillation and compromise. This was true not only of the Szechuan students but of those from other places and of intellectuals in general. As a matter of fact only a very few of those who cut a brilliant figure in the revolutionary struggles of that time persisted to the end. This demonstrates the need for intellectuals to continually remould themselves and improve their thinking in order to march with the times.

8. THE FOUNDING OF CHINA REVOLUTIONARY LEAGUE

In 1905 not only was the revolutionary movement in full swing in China, but, under the influence of the Russian revolution, a revolutionary tide swept over the entire East, a condition which was highly favourable to China. The Chinese movement, which was spreading and increasing in vigour, was in urgent need of a unified and centralized leadership. Such organizations as the secret societies and religious sects had become outdated and were unable to shoulder the responsibility of leading the bourgeois revolution. The time for the birth of a proletarian political party was far from ripe, and a bourgeois political party was the only one suitable to the existing social conditions. Many small revolutionary bodies such as the Society for the Revival of China, the Restoration Society and the Society for the Revival of the Chinese Nation, somewhat akin to bourgeois political parties in nature, were already in existence. The problem was how to unite them into one body, produce a clearly defined programme and enable it to be put into concerted action. The China Revolutionary League filled the bill, and the birth of this league was the fulfilment of a historical necessity.

Among the small revolutionary bodies mentioned above, the first to be organized was the Society for the Revival of China headed by Dr. Sun Yat-sen. Dr. Sun was born into a peasant family in Chungshan County, Kwangtung, in 1866, and came under the influence of the Taiping Revolution when he was only a boy. This was one of the reasons why he later advocated the principle of the equalization of landownership. When he grew older he went to live with his elder brother in Honolulu where he entered school. His brother was bourgeois and the school where he studied was also bourgeois. Under such conditions he was easily influenced by Western bourgeois ideas. In 1894, he wrote a letter to Li Hung-chang, advising him to do something in the way of political reform; this did not bring any results. After the outbreak of the Sino-Japanese War in 1894 Dr. Sun Yat-sen, disgusted with the corruption of the Ching government, began to engage in revolutionary activities. He organized the Society for the Revival of China in Honolulu and with the help of some secret societies, staged an uprising in Canton in 1895. In spite of ruthless persecution by the reactionary Ching government, his influence on the people, especially overseas Chinese and those studying abroad, steadily increased as the revolutionary situation developed. The capitalists among the overseas Chinese were oppressed by the foreign imperialists and had little connection with the feudal force at home. They constituted a special section of the Chinese bourgeoisie and had stronger revolutionary leanings. It was precisely the political stand of this section of the Chinese bourgeoisie that Dr. Sun Yat-sen rep-

72

resented. After the failure of the Yi Ho Tuan Movement he became more energetic in his revolutionary activities. In 1904 he brought forward a programme to "drive out the Manchus, revive the Chinese nation, establish a republic and equalize landownership". This marked another forward step in his thinking.

The Restoration Society was a small revolutionary group founded by Tsai Yuan-pei, Chang Tai-yen and Tao Cheng-chang in 1904. It strongly advocated national revolution and represented the long-cherished desire of the people in southern China to overthrow the rule of the Manchus and restore China to the Hans. The aim advocated by this society conformed to the national interests of the working people and the bour-geoisie and was also supported by those Han landlords who were hostile to the Manchus. Consequently its influence was strongest in the lower reaches of the Yangtse River and among the Chinese students studying in Japan. The Society for the Revival of the Chinese Nation was also founded in 1904 by Huang Hsing, Chen Tien-hua, Sung Chiao-jen and Liu Kuei-yi. Its members, youthful intellectuals, were mainly Chinese students studying in Japan. It had some connections with the secret societies. Its base was in Hunan, and the society rep-resented the newly arisen bourgeoisie of that province in their demand for economic development. Neither of the two societies had a clearly defined or complete programme nor did they have any strict organization. They were all of a local character and therefore could not lead the nation-wide rev-olutionary movement which was daily increasing in strength.

In July 1905 Dr. Sun Yat-sen returned to Japan from Europe. He advocated the unity of all revolutionary forces as well as of all small revolutionary groups in China and took active steps to prepare for the organization of the China Revolu-tionary League. On August 13, the Chinese students in Tokyo held a big meeting at Fujimiro Restaurant to welcome him. More than 1,000 people attended. The room, the corridors and even the door-steps of the building were crowded with people. His fiery speech evoked wave after wave of applause. It made people realize the correctness of the revolutionary path and the danger of reformism. On August 20 the China Revolutionary League was founded, after which its statutes and organization gradually took shape. In October the *Min Pao (People's Journal)*, organ of the league, began publication. Its first issue carried an introduction, written by Dr. Sun Yat-sen, which enunciated the programme and principle of the league much clearer than ever before. The statutes of the league stated that the aim of the league was to "drive out the Manchus, revive the Chinese nation, establish a republic and equalize landownership". In his introductory remarks to the *People's Journal*, Dr. Sun also put forward the People's Three Principles — the principle of nationalism, the principle of democracy and the principle of the people's livelihood. Thus the league had mapped out a comparatively complete programme for the bourgeois revolution. It unequivocally called for the total overthrow of the reactionary Ching government which had been in power for over two hundred years and drew a clear line between the revolutionaries and the reformers. It called for the total overthrow of the over two-thousand-year-old feudal system of absolute monarchy and for the establishment of a republic. This was a big step forward compared with the simple idea of overthrowing the Manchus and restoring China to the Hans. It also called for the equalization of landownership as a means of solving the land problem and preventing the development of capitalism in China. The idea of preventing the development of capitalism was merely a flight of the imagination without scientific basis. Dr. Sun Yat-sen put forward this principle out of concern for the miserable life of the toiling masses and sympathy with the exploited. This subjective socialist idea was to a certain degree a reflection of the noble spirit and noble ideal of the Chinese people. But in effect, the programme of the Revolutionary League drawn up by Dr. Sun Yat-sen was fundamentally a programme for the establishment of a bourgeois

republic.   Under the conditions then prevailing it indicated
significant social progress. This programme gave the bourgeois
revolutionaries the most powerful weapon they had ever had,
and enabled them to score one victory after another in their
struggle against the bourgeois reformers.

The various departments of the Revolutionary League were
gradually set up. The extremely cruel rule of the Ching government forced the league to conduct all its activities in the
greatest secrecy and adopt many of the methods traditionally
used by the secret societies. For instance, its secret slogans,
though differing in content from those used by the secret
societies, were similar in form, being in fact copied from
them.   The organizational form of the league was mainly
an imitation of the bourgeois governments and political
parties of the West. The league's headquarters, for example, was headed by a premier. Under him, there were three
departments — legislative, executive and judicial — obviously
copied from bourgeois government organization.   The fact
that it had a new political programme and organizational
form marked the fundamental difference between the
Revolutionary League and the backward, feudal secret
societies and religious sects of the past.   It was the first
bourgeois political party of China to have been so well
organized.

Because I was comparatively well-known among the Chinese
students in Japan, especially among the Szechuan students, I
was elected a member of the league's legislative department.
Although this department was the league's highest organ of
power, it seldom carried out any activities. This was partly
because circumstances did not permit frequent secret activities. A still more important reason was that the Revolutionary League, being by nature a bourgeois political party,
had a rather loose organization. It was founded on the basis
of three small political groups, the Society for the Revival of
China, the Restoration Society and the Society for the Revival
of the Chinese Nation, and had a rather mixed membership.

Its members consisted of workers and peasants (mainly members of old secret societies), intellectuals, capitalists and those landlords who were against the Manchus. Thus it may be said that the league was an anti-Manchu national confederation made up of all classes with the bourgeoisie in the leadership. It was in reality a united front organization. Unfortunately, the differences between the small bodies which made up the league were never entirely obliterated, and there were frequent dissensions among its members. Chiu Chin and Hsu Hsi-lin, for instance, were members of the Restoration Society. Chiu Chin joined the league, became a member of the league's legislative department and head of the league's branch in Chekiang. Hsu Hsi-lin resolutely refused to join the league. In the uprising which they staged later, Chiu Chin had, on the one hand, to talk to Hsu Hsi-lin and other members of the Restoration Society as a member of that society, and on the other, to talk with members of the Revolutionary League as a member of that league. Chang Tai-yen and Sung Chiao-jen did not give due credence to the leadership of Dr. Sun Yat-sen. All this showed the inherent weakness of the Revolutionary League as a bourgeois organization and brewed the crises that caused the failure of the Revolution of 1911.

9. THE PROTEST AGAINST THE "SUPERVISORY REGULATIONS"

After the founding of the Revolutionary League the centre of revolutionary activities was in Japan; the Ching government therefore requested the Japanese imperialist government to suppress the activities of the Chinese students studying there. In November 1905 the Japanese government announced the "Regulations for the Supervision of Chinese and Korean Students Studying in Japan". This aroused the indignation of the Chinese students who at once protested strongly against these "supervisory regulations".

Dr. Sun Yat-sen, leader of
the China Revolutionary League

The Japanese imperialists were double-faced and even multi-faced in their aggression against China. On the one hand they supported the reactionary Ching government while on the other they supported the revolutionary movement. When supporting reaction they would foster two or more members of the ruling circle as their agents. When supporting the revolutionaries they would bolster up several groups at the same time. In this way, they thought, at whatever time and whoever was in power, Japan could exert its aggressive influence through its agents. Before and during the Russo-Japanese War of 1904 Japan tried its best to win over the Chinese students studying in that country, and the Chinese students did feel sympathetic towards Japan at that time. After the end of the war, however, Japan turned against the Chinese students and, working hand in glove with the reactionary Ching government, began to suppress the students' revolutionary activities. This provoked the resistance of the students. A certain member of the Japanese Diet made a most absurd and impertinent statement, suggesting that the Japanese empire should include three regions contained within three circles with Tokyo as the centre. The first circle should include Korea, the second, northeastern China and the third, all the rest of China. This audacious statement infuriated the Chinese students. All these events provoked the Chinese students to launch the struggle against the "supervisory regulations".

The publication of the "supervisory regulations" made the Chinese students so angry that they decided not to tolerate this humiliation and to return to China at once. This decision, made during a flush of anger and excitement, was difficult to implement. Having made the decision, the students realized that they would be a laughing-stock to the Japanese imperialists if they did not carry it out. Chen Tien-hua, a Chinese patriot, aware of this and indignant at the irresponsible leadership of the Association of Chinese Students Studying in Japan, committed suicide by throwing himself into the sea. He hoped that his action would inspire the students to persist in their struggle. Chen Tien-hua was a pioneer in China's bourgeois democratic revolution and an outstanding revolutionary propagandist. His pamphlets written in the vernacular, such as *Wake Up! Alarm Bell*, and the *Lion's Roar*, were very widely circulated and played a great agitational role among the people. His last words earnestly urged the Chinese students in Japan to persist in their struggle. In his letter to the executive secretaries of the Association of Chinese Students Studying in Japan he wrote: "I've heard that some of you have resigned. I don't know why. The situation has become critical. You do not try to do your best, but resign. Does this not aggravate the humiliation of the Chinese students studying in Japan?" This letter moved many people, but it had no effect on the obdurate top leaders of the association, who were afraid to commit themselves. At that time I was one of the executive secretaries of the association and I did whatever I could to keep things going. At one of the meetings of the association a speech was made by Hu Ying which was greatly appreciated by the members. Learning that he was connected with the *People's Journal*, organ of the Revolutionary League, they elected him leader of the organization fighting against the "supervisory regulations". At that time the Revolutionary League worked underground but the *People's Journal* was published openly. Working with the *People's Journal* therefore implied membership in the league. The fact that the students gave their hearty support to Hu Ying showed the great prestige the Revolutionary League enjoyed among the masses.

The organization to fight against the "supervisory regulations" had gone into action. However, it was extremely difficult to lead some 10,000 scattered students in a strike and to organize their return to China. There were big problems to be faced, such as where were the travel expenses to come from, and what were the students going to do after their return home. These problems had to be solved. In spite of various difficulties many students did return to China, including Chiu Chin, the famous woman revolutionary. The students who returned from Japan were subjected to the dual tactics of persecution and enticement by the Ching government. It carried out arrests amongst the revolutionaries and at the same time sought to win over returned students by allowing them to take special examinations for official advancement. Many students actually fell into this trap, took the examination, accepted official positions and became docile servants of the reactionary Ching government.

Suddenly when the students were returning to China en masse there appeared in Tokyo an "association for the maintenance of order" among the Chinese students. A statement was made by the association to the effect that those who did not want to return to China could continue their stay in Japan while those who wanted to return could do so if they wished. The association was organized by Chinese students studying in Hosei University and Wang Ching-wei[1] was among those who signed the statement. When the students read the statement they were surprised and did not know what had prompted it. This was what had happened. Dr. Sun Yat-sen sent a telegram to the Chinese students in Japan saying that he did not approve of all the Chinese students' returning to China. He was afraid that if the members of the Revolutionary League returned en masse they might be mass arrested by the Ching government. In this Dr. Sun was entirely right. He made us realize that the decision for all students to return to China, though made under the spell of justified anger, was not feasible and should be changed. When Wang Ching-wei re-

---

[1] Wang Ching-wei was one of the leaders of the China Revolutionary League but later became a turncoat and traitor. In 1937 the Japanese imperialists started a war of aggression against China. In December 1938 Wang Ching-wei openly surrendered to them and in March 1940 became president of the puppet Central Government of Nanking. He died in Japan in November 1944.

ceived the telegram he did not consult any one else and, without discussing it with the students, rashly organized an "association for the maintenance of order". In doing this Wang Ching-wei was entirely wrong. It is possible that Wang Ching-wei carried out Dr. Sun Yat-sen's instructions in this way because of cowardice. He was an impulsive but spineless man, irresolute, easy to change, and liable to blow hot and cold. Although these bad characteristics of Wang Ching-wei were already perceivable, he did have some "prestige" among the students. Eloquent in speech, pleasant in features and capable of writing excellent agitational articles, he deceived quite a large number of people. Besides, he had Dr. Sun Yat-sen's instructions on hand, and with this authority it was easy for him to get a hearing when he asked for "maintenance of order".

The Chinese students' struggle against the "supervisory regulations" gained the just sympathy of international public opinion. It created a great disturbance in Japanese political circles, the parties out of office using this as a pretext for launching strong attacks against the party in power. In order to lessen the pressure of world public opinion and to cope with the attacks launched by the opposition parties, thereby consolidating its own position, the party in power sent men to negotiate with the Association of Chinese Students Studying in Japan. The leading members of the association, however, had all left the headquarters and the remaining few people who were working in the office of the association did nothing but complain. Under such conditions I felt that it was my duty to shoulder the responsibility. When I was a small boy my grandmother used to tell me that "it is easy to spread a feast but difficult to tidy things up after the feast". She also told me that in doing anything one must go through with it from start to finish. She said that "a man who gives up a thing before it is finished will have no future". I have never allowed myself to forget these words. I always liked to do the work of tidying-up. Some people predicted that I had a "hard fate", but I am not depressed because I believe that it is only by fighting against a "hard fate" that a person can win final victory in life. In my home province people used to say that in eating the sugar-cane you should start from the top and go down to the root end, for in that way the cane tastes sweeter and sweeter; if you go from the root to the top the cane tastes less and less sweet. I considered this saying as quite philosophical, for sweetness after bitterness is the happiest thing in life. Consequently, I was not at all discouraged by the distressing condition of the association. On the contrary I felt even more enthusiastic. I always went to the office of the association once or twice a week to encourage the people there to persist to the end in their work. Owing to our continuous struggle the Japanese government finally granted ten or more of our demands. The Japanese government which had refused to give its recognition to the Association of Chinese Students Studying in Japan was at last compelled to do so. Thus the vigorous struggle against the "supervisory regulations" ended with a certain degree of success.

10. THE STRUGGLE BETWEEN THE REVOLUTIONARIES AND THE REFORMERS

The China Revolutionary League was formed on the basis of the steadily spreading revolutionary movement. In turn, the founding of the league gave impetus to the revolutionary movement.

People of practically every social stratum joined the movement or were at least influenced by it. The working class, though still in the initial stage of its development, also launched many spontaneous struggles. In 1905 the workers of Shanghai held several strikes to protest against the dismissal of workers and wage cuts. In 1906 there was a continuous chain of strikes in Shanghai. The weavers in Hangchow also went on strike. At that time the workers used very simple methods of struggle.

In April 1905, for example, the workers of Yangshupu, Shanghai, held a strike during which they smashed the machines in the factory. This showed that the workers of those days had no real class consciousness. However, as the struggle between the Chinese workers and capitalists continued, it was inevitable that the workers would gradually become class conscious and able to fulfil their great historic mission.

In 1906 many places in the Yangtse River valley were plagued by famine and the peasants' struggle in that region became very intense. Peasant uprisings occurred in Szechuan and Kweichow in the upper reaches of the Yangtse, in Hunan and Kiangsi in the middle reaches, and in Anhwei and Kiangsu in the lower reaches. In addition, the peasants in Honan in northern China and in Kwangsi in southern China were also waging incessant struggles. The anti-church struggle, which had quietened down after the failure of the Yi Ho Tuan Movement, again became active. The famous Nanchang church incident was an example. In 1906 a French missionary brutally murdered Chiang Shao-tang, the magistrate of Nanchang County, a comparatively upright man among the officials of the Ching government. This aroused public indignation and the people beat the missionary to death and burned the French church which he used as his centre. The French, British and American imperialists, defying all reason, sent gunboats into Poyang Lake to threaten the Chinese people. The people throughout the country seethed with anger. When Hsu Teh-li,[1] then a teacher in Changsha, heard about the gunboats he made a speech to the students of his school, during which he became so excited that he took a

[1] Hsu Teh-li is now member of the Central Committee of the Chinese Communist Party and also member of the Standing Committee of the National People's Congress.

cleaver and cut off one of his fingers, swearing that he would wreak vengeance on the enemy. A reformist by the name of Peng Kuo-chun who was present at the meeting used Hsu's blood to write the words "Please convene a parliament!" Thus the blood of a patriot was utilized by a reformist as a means to realize his personal ambition. Simultaneously, struggles against the churches, which were imperialist tools, were also carried out in many parts of the country including Anhwei, Fukien, Chekiang and Szechuan.

Inspired by the extensive struggles of workers and peasants a new campaign for the right to build railways and open mines was launched by the people of various provinces. This struggle was directed mainly against the foreign imperialists. It was patriotic in nature, with the people taking part in it belonging to many different classes and strata. They included an enormous number of working people and also members of the bourgeoisie and intellectuals who were particularly active. Its influence also spread to certain persons of the upper ruling class. After a prolonged and complicated struggle the people of Hunan, Hupeh, Kiangsu, Chekiang, Anhwei, Shantung, Shansi, Honan and Szechuan succeeded, to a certain extent, in restoring or maintaining their right to build railways and open mines. In 1900 the right to build the Canton-Hankow Railway was stolen by the American-China Development Company. In 1905 it was recovered. The Szechuan-Hankow Railway was also changed into a private enterprise because of the strong pressure of the Szechuan people. In order to resist British and French aggression the people of Szechuan had long wished to build the Szechuan-Hankow Railway themselves. Greatly annoyed by the lack of modern transport facilities in their province, the Szechuan students studying in Japan felt an urgent need for the Szechuan people themselves to build the railway. In 1904 they sent a telegram to the provincial authorities of Szechuan in which they outlined the concrete measure of raising a fund from the sale of shares to build the Szechuan-Hankow Railway. To set an example they promised to buy more than 300,000 taels worth of shares. Meanwhile they published an open letter to the people of Szechuan warning them of the danger of the country being ruined by the imperialists if they lost their right to build railways and warning them of the necessity to build these railways by their own effort. In 1905 the rules for the raising of a fund through the issuance of shares for building the Szechuan-Hankow Railway were published. According to these rules no shares would be sold to foreigners and no loans would be accepted from them. The shares were to be bought by landowners, on the basis of 3 per cent of all rent collected, and by the provincial government with increased revenue from the *likin*, a special tax, which ultimately came from the people too. Thus, in one way or another, all the people of Szechuan were connected with the building of the Szechuan-Hankow Railway. Unfortunately, the Szechuan-Hankow Railway Company eventually came entirely under government control. The shares allotted to the government were never paid for and the private shares were gradually embezzled. Towards the end of 1906 the Szechuan students in Japan issued a joint statement denouncing the government for monopolizing the control of the company and demanded that the building of the railway be entrusted to a private enterprise. The railway company then fell into the hands of the gentry who supported a constitutional monarchy. Later when the Ching government tried to nationalize the railway it was opposed not only by all the people of Szechuan but also by the gentry who, for their own interests, joined the people in their struggle. This was how, on the eve of the Revolution of 1911, the railway agitation of Szechuan became a movement of all the people.

The revolutionary upsurge, marked by the founding of the China Revolutionary League, made the Ching government aware that its very existence was seriously threatened. In 1906 it was therefore compelled to announce its intention of forming a constitutional government, thereby hoping to lessen the people's revolutionary enthusiasm. The struggle between the revolutionaries led by Dr. Sun Yat-sen and the reformers led by Kang Yu-wei and Liang Chi-chao became sharper. This was an inevitable reflection of the sharpening class struggle. The *People's Journal*, organ of the revolutionaries, and the *New People's Journal*, organ of the reformers, engaged in a bitter uncompromising battle. Under the cloak of patriotism the *New People's Journal* propagated monarchism. It said that revolution would lead to an internecine war and the partitioning of the country by foreign powers, that China must have a constitutional monarchy preceded by a transitional stage of an "enlightened monarchy" under the Ching government. It denounced the equalization of landownership as a measure designed to profit only beggars and vagabonds, claiming that its practice would ruin the social order. The *People's Journal* vigorously refuted these fallacious arguments. It explained in detail why it was necessary to overthrow the Ching government, pointing out that the Ching regime was betraying the country and that all patriotic people should strive to overthrow it. Furthermore, it stated that China could hope to survive only by overthrowing the Ching government by revolutionary means and by establishing a democratic republic. The journal held that the outworn ideas about "enlightened monarchy" and "constitutional monarchy" were meant to help the Ching government to perpetuate its criminal rule. It also pointed out that land must be nationalized so as to eliminate the wide gap between the poor and the rich. Under the vigorous attack of the *People's Journal*, the *New People's Journal* suffered a complete defeat which led to the cessation of its publication. Despite serious defects, the programme of the Revolutionary League took a more definite form due to the polemics waged by the *People's Journal*. The attack was directed solely against the Manchu ruling class while imperialism, the real enemy of the Chinese nation, was ignored. The six principles of the *People's Journal*[1] show that there were still illusions about the role of the imperialists, especially the Japanese imperialists. Furthermore, while the *People's Journal* gave wide publicity to the glorious tradition of the Han people, it failed to direct its main attack against feudalism, the people's real enemy within the country. Therefore, it was unable to satisfactorily refute the *New People's Journal* arguments that revolution would lead to civil war and to the partitioning of China by foreign countries. Obviously, the feeble bourgeoisie of China was unable to put forward a clear anti-imperialist, anti-feudal revolutionary programme. Thus the glorious task of putting forward such a programme had to be undertaken later by the great working class of China.

When the controversy between the *People's Journal* and the *New People's Journal* was in full swing, nearly all the Chinese students in Japan took part in it. I remember one winter day in 1906, when a group of Szechuan students held a discussion in their dormitory. Most of them were in favour of revolution. Chou Hsien-teng, originally a good friend of mine, alone stood for constitutional monarchy. While he was talking vociferously someone threw a brazier at him. He was so frightened that he ran away like a mouse before a cat. This incident, small though it was, reflected the political failure of the reformers.

Kang Yu-wei, Liang Chi-chao and their party, however, did not take their failure lying down. When the Ching government pretended to make preparations for a constitutional government they were beside themselves with joy. They took active steps to organize a party for the support of the constitutional monarchy and prepared to return to China as hon-

---

[1] The six principles of the *People's Journal* were as follows: (1) overthrow the present corrupt government; (2) establish a republican government; (3) nationalize the land; (4) struggle for real peace in the world; (5) stand for unity between the Chinese and Japanese peoples; (6) request foreign countries to support China's work of modernization.

oured pioneers of constitutionalism within the Ching government. Originally the dispute between the revolutionaries and constitutional monarchists, that is, the reformers, was in the main theoretical. It now became a struggle for action. In July 1907 the *Cheng Wen Sheh* (Political Association), founded by Liang Chi-chao, held its inaugural meeting in the Kinki Hostel. During the meeting members of the Revolutionary League physically assaulted Liang Chi-chao, while the Szechuan students grabbed his underling Pai Chien (Szechuanese) seriously wounding him. This violent action, widely acclaimed, demonstrated the unpopularity of the constitutional monarchists. After that incident the constitutional monarchists lost the sympathy of the people and could only recruit supporters from the upper stratum of the gentry.

11.   ABORTIVE ARMED UPRISINGS

The revolutionary movement began to sweep over the whole country, but the Revolutionary League failed to give competent leadership to this magnificent struggle of the people of all strata, especially of the broad masses of workers and peasants. It devoted most of its energy to organizing armed uprisings, hoping to overthrow the reactionary rule of the Ching government by military strength alone. From 1906 to 1908 it launched a whole series of armed uprisings.

The members of the Revolutionary League who had returned to China from Japan, as a result of their protest against "supervisory regulations", became active organizers of armed uprisings. For examlpe, Liu Tao-yi after his return to Hunan enlisted the help of the secret societies and carried out revolutionary activities in the border areas between Hunan and Kiangsi Provinces. Towards the end of 1906 the famous Pinghsiang-Liling-Liuyang Uprising took place, 6,000 workers from the Anyuan Colliery being the main force behind the uprising. These miners were not yet class conscious but instinctively took part in the uprising. However, the honour must go to them for writing the first page in the history of the revolutionary struggle of the Chinese working class.

At the beginning of 1907, at the request of the Ching government, the Japanese imperialists deported the revolutionaries and Dr. Sun Yat-sen was forced to leave Japan for Indo-China (now Viet Nam). He set up revolutionary headquarters in Hanoi for the direction of military activities. Subsequently, uprisings occurred in Chaochow, Huichow, Chinchow and Lienchow. These uprisings failed, and Dr. Sun, together with Huang Hsing, another leader of the Revolutionary League, planned to attack Chennankuan (now Munankuan) from Indo-China, take that town and then march forward into Kwangsi Province. An uprising was therefore launched in Chennankuan on the Chinese border near Indo-China.

Dr. Sun Yat-sen was organizing uprisings in Kwangtung and Kwangsi. Hsu Hsi-lin, a member of the Restoration Society, acting independently of the Revolutionary League, assassinated En Ming, governor of Anhwei Province, in Anking in the summer of 1907, and staged an uprising. Chiu Chin also planned to take action in Shaohsing, Chekiang Province. The Anking uprising failed and Hsu Hsi-lin was executed. Chiu Chin was also arrested and died a martyr. Chiu Chin, a great heroine in modern Chinese history, gave her life for national liberation and for the emancipation of Chinese women. She was a model woman revolutionary during the period of the old-democratic revolution in China.

After the failure of the Chennankuan uprising Dr. Sun Yat-sen and Huang Hsing planned to launch another uprising in the border area of Yunnan. The Revolutionary League had paid a great deal of attention to the border area of Yunnan because of the British imperialists' aggression against Hpimaw. It frequently sent members, especially those from Yunnan and Szechuan, to work in that region. Due to the league's revolutionary work in Yunnan, Dr. Sun Yat-sen and Huang Hsing decided to launch an uprising there. In March 1908 an uprising occurred in Hokou, Yunnan. When the news of this uprising reached Japan the league members in Tokyo were encouraged; they decided to immediately send a number of people to Hokou as reinforcement. Unfortunately when these people arrived in Hanoi, they learned that the uprising had failed, and they had to return to Tokyo.

After the movement against the "supervisory regulations" Hsieh Feng-chi and Hsiung Keh-wu, members of the Revolutionary League from Szechuan, also returned to China to make active preparations for armed uprisings. The planned 1907 Chengtu uprising failed before it was launched and six of its leaders were arrested and imprisoned. This incident was a blow to the whole province of Szechuan. Hsieh Feng-chi then planned to launch an uprising in Hsufu. News of the plan leaked out and he was arrested and died heroically. Hsieh displayed a truly courageous and loyal spirit after his arrest and Chao Fan, the provincial judge of Szechuan, was so moved that he resigned from his post when he found that he was unable to save Hsieh from death. This resignation indicates that at that time even some of the more enlightened Ching officials felt the irresistible power of the revolutionary current. In 1908 Hsiung Keh-wu again went to Japan. We bought some fire-arms to help him stage uprisings. These were sent to Chungchow, Szechuan, where they were entrusted to a certain member of the Revolutionary League for safe keeping. Unfortunately, the Ching government got news of this. Afraid of bringing disaster to his family, he threw the fire-arms into the river. In the spring of 1909 the Kwangan uprising launched by Hsiung Keh-wu and others failed and Hsiung fled to Shanghai. In 1911 the Revolutionary League launched an uprising in Canton on a larger scale using most of its ablest members, but the uprising also failed and the losses were extremely heavy.

All the armed uprisings launched by the Revolutionary League failed because of the severe suppressive measures carried out by the reactionary Ching government. This demonstrates that painstaking efforts must first be made to mobilize the masses before launching an uprising. Only when the people's revolutionary enthusiasm has reached its height can they be led to start an armed uprising. All-round and careful preparations must be made. It is only when all the necessary subjective and objective conditions have been obtained that an uprising can be launched with the possibility of success. All armed uprisings which are divorced from the revolutionary struggle of the masses are but military opportunism. A military struggle that is waged without careful preparation is adventurism. All opportunist and adventurist actions are doomed to failure. Yet although the many armed uprisings launched under the leadership of the Revolutionary League failed, they dealt a serious blow to the reactionary rule of the Ching government. At the same time they inspired and encouraged the broad masses of people to resolutely join the struggle against the reactionary Ching rule. They proved to the people, with hard facts, that only by armed revolution could the reactionary Ching rule be overthrown and that all other means would prove futile. Countless numbers of heroes and patriots laid down their lives in the uprisings. They did not hesitate to shed their blood and give up everything in the struggle for their motherland's bright future. Their dauntless revolutionary spirit has written glorious pages in the history of the Chinese people and set an example worthy to be sung and followed for all time.

12. THE SZECHUAN MAGAZINE

The reactionary Ching government, in addition to ruthlessly suppressing revolutionary uprisings, also strictly prohibited and sabotaged all kinds of revolutionary propaganda. After 1906 it became increasingly difficult to send copies of the *People's Journal* to China. So the revolutionaries of the various provinces among the Chinese students in Japan began to publish new magazines or re-edit old ones. They published them under the names of their own provinces, and sent them back to China in small quantities, thus carrying out revolutionary propaganda. This was how the *Yunnan Review* was published. At that time the people of the whole country were struggling against the British imperialist aggression against Hpimaw at the Yunnan border. The *Yunnan Review* laid great emphasis on foreign aggression, which made it easier to enter China and increased its popularity among the readers. The *Szechuan Magazine* was published under similar conditions.

Lui Tieh-yai, Teng Hsieh and others had previously published a magazine called *Cuckoo's Call*, which thoroughly exposed the evil and corruption of the county government of Pingshan, Szechuan. Although its articles dealing with provincial and national affaires were outspoken, they did not go very deep. In the latter half of 1907 the students from Szechuan decided to expand the *Cuckoo's Call* into a new magazine called the *Szechuan Magazine* and entrusted me with the work of editing and publishing. I finished my studies in the Seijo School in 1906 and entered the No. 6 High School in Okayama, which was a government preparatory school for colleges. I studied in its department of technology. Having now been entitled to government support, I had no problem of tuition fees. I had been in the school for one year when I was charged with the task of running the *Szechuan Magazine*. It took me at least half a day to travel by train from Okayama to Tokyo, so I had to stop studying if I wanted to work for the magazine. On the pretext of poor health, I asked the school authorities to give me leave of absence for one year. This was granted and enabled me to devote all my time to revolutionary work. I rented a fairly big house for the *Szechuan Magazine*, which was later used both as a publishing house and as a centre for revolutionary activities. Lui Tieh-yai and Teng Hsieh also joined the editorial board. Towards the end of 1907, after a short period of preparation, the *Szechuan Magazine* appeared as a journal of a highly revolutionary character. It was warmly received by its readers and enjoyed a wide circulation, every issue having to be reprinted to meet the demands. The *Szechuan Magazine* was characterized by its resolute opposition to imperialism and the reactionary Ching rule, and its firm revolutionary stand. Unfortunately only three issues of the magazine were published, because the Japanese government confiscated the fourth issue and forced the office of the *Szechuan Magazine* to close. A survey of the contents of the magazine shows that an enormous amount of space was given to articles dealing with the following subjects: the British imperialists' aggression in China's Tibet; the British and French imperialists' aggression in Yunnan; the Japanese imperialists' aggression against Korea and northeastern China; the crimes of the reactionary Ching government, its persecution of the people and betrayal of the nation; encouraging the people to struggle for the right to build railways and to carry out revolutionary struggle. Even the poems it carried had a deep patriotic content and sentimental themes were avoided. The general tenor of the magazine was patriotic, democratic and, to an extent, anarchistic. Needless to say, the patriotism of those days was comparatively simple and abstract. It was not the socialist patriotism of today which is profound and rich in content. The only democracy we could talk about in those days was bourgeois democracy which was rather narrow. Anarchism, as everyone knows, is, from the standpoint of a communist, a reactionary idea. But, at that time, as it encouraged people to carry out dangerous revolutionary struggles it played mainly a progressive role. It should be noted, however, that anarchism also had a negative effect, giving rise to hero worship and contempt for the masses. On the whole we may say that at the time of its appearance, the *Szechuan Magazine* was one of the most revolutionary and progressive publications.

In the period from 1906 to 1908, certain wavering people became disheartened because of the failure of the armed uprisings launched by the Revolutionary League. At that time the Revolutionary League in Japan was loosely organized. Sun Yat-sen, Huang Hsing and other leaders did not visit Japan very often, and without leadership the league was like a heap of sand. I decided to make frequent contacts with the league members from various provinces and often held meetings with them. In this way real contact was maintained with responsible provincial league members, this prevented the dissolution of the league, and enabled it to persist in revolutionary struggle. Owing to the increasingly critical situation in China many revolutionaries in secret societies including my eldest brother fled the country and went to Japan. One day I had a talk with Chiao Ta-feng and some other members of the league. "The league has recently," I said, "been busying itself with preparations for uprisings and has practically forgotten the secret societies. Since many members of the secret societies from various provinces are now in Japan why not merge the secret societies of the whole country." This suggestion was gladly accepted by all those league members who in the past had connections with the secret societies. They knew that the potential revolutionary strength of the lower social strata was very great. My eldest brother, who had a high standing in the Society of Brothers in Szechuan, on my recommendation now became a member of the Revolutionary League. He was very pleased with my idea of a merger. In the latter half of 1907, through the assiduous effort of the league members, the leaders of the secret societies — the Society of Brothers, the Society of Filial Piety and Fraternity, the Triple Society, and the Triad Society — organized in Japan the Kung Chin Hui or the Society for Mutual Progress. Chang Pai-hsiang, leader of the Society of Filial Piety and Fraternity, was elected president of the new society, because as a senior member of the secret society, he was familiar with its responsible personnel in many places and had a big following in eastern Szechuan. In addition to Chang, Chiao Ta-feng and Sun Wu were also leaders of the Society for Mutual Progress. At a later date they succeeded in establishing close relations with the secret societies in Hupeh and Hunan Provinces. The Society for Mutual Progress stood for the same principles as those of the Revolutionary League but it laid more stress on anti-Manchu propaganda. Considering that many of the top leaders of the secret societies came from landlord families or had close ties with the landlord class, the Society for Mutual Progress changed the slogan of "equalization of land-ownership" into "equalization of human rights" so that it might be easily accepted by all of them. Later, certain leaders of the Society for Mutual Progress, in defending this change, said that the latter slogan has a much broader concept and that it was much more suitable for propaganda among members of secret societies. But facts proved that because the society abandoned the original slogan, it was impossible to attract the broad masses of peasants. There-fore, in making the change the society had really committed a mistake of far-reaching consequences. The society's prog-ramme had serious defects. Its organization was loose and its component societies carried out activities independently, without following any central, unified leadership. In spite of this, however, it succeeded in rallying most of the secret societies in southern China against the Manchus. With its comparatively broad, popular basis it helped to spread the revolutionary movement and strengthened the Revolution-ary League.

After the Society for Mutual Progress was organized I again concentrated my efforts on the work of the Revolu-tionary League and the *Szechuan Magazine*. As this magazine carried out both revolutionary propaganda and organizational work, it suffered the same persecution by the reactionary Ching government as did the *People's Journal*.

In 1908 the Ching government sent Tang Shao-yi to the United States as a special envoy. While passing through Japan Tang, acting on the instructions of the Ching government, requested the Japanese government to ban the *People's Journal* and the *Szechuan Magazine*. Consequently, Chang Tai-yen, editor of the *People's Journal*, and I were both involved in a lawsuit. The *People's Journal* was accused of "encouraging assassinations and endangering public security". The journal was banned and fines were inflicted. The Japanese imperialists purposely made the case against the *Szechuan Magazine* even more serious, inflicted a larger fine and sentenced me to six months' imprisonment. This was how it happened. After the summer vacation of 1908 my year's leave was up and I had to go back to Okayama to continue my studies. It was agreed that my duties as editor and publisher of the *Szechuan Magazine* be transferred to Liao Hsi-hsien, member of the Revolutionary League and president of the Association of Szechuan Students Studying in Japan. When the lawsuit was brought up against the *Szechuan Magazine* Liao should have gone to court for the trial, but he refused and shifted the responsibility to me. People thought that he was unfair. As an old saying goes, when you see a right thing and do not do it you lack courage. What is there to be afraid of in going to court? I decided to stand trial myself, people admired my decision and engaged Sakurae, a famous Japanese lawyer, to be my counsel. On the day of the trial I went to the court quite calmly. Many people wanted to attend the trial but the court declared that the case was a serious one and the public would not be admitted. The people were very indignant and were worried about me, yet they could do nothing but wait outside for the result of the trial. When the trial began, the public prosecutor charged me with four great "offences": 1) advocating revolution, 2) encouraging assassination, 3) instigating Japanese colonies to oppose the "empire", and 4) opposing the Tenno.[1] When the judge mentioned the word "Tenno" he made gestures to show his deference to the emperor which were rather funny. Sakurae did not come that day but sent another lawyer to be my counsel. "To advocate revolution against the Ching government in a foreign country is not a crime," said my counsel. "The publication of anarchist articles cannot be said to be an encouragement to assassination. The third and fourth charges are of course undeniable. But as the articles were reprinted from other sources due to carelessness in editing, they should be regarded as a misconduct rather than an offence." After having debated the question for some time the court was adjourned. About half an hour later the trial was resumed and the judge pronounced the verdict. As "the evidence proved the defendant to be guilty" the judge said that the magazine was banned. A fine of 100 yen was fixed as a penalty for offence, and the editor-publisher of the magazine was sentenced to six months' imprisonment. Then he added that because the culprit was still a student he was reprieved. Thus the incident ended. When I left the court the people who were waiting outside cheered. I told them all that had happened. They realized that the Japanese imperialists were working hand in glove with the Ching government and were trying to suppress the Chinese revolution. The so-called trial, defence and verdict were nothing but a hocus-pocus.

---

[1] The *Szechuan Magazine* was accused of opposing the Japanese emperor on account of a news report on the "red flag incident" which was carried in the fourth issue of the magazine. The "red flag incident" happened on June 22, 1908. On this day various groups of Japanese socialists and anarchists held a meeting in the Kinki Hostel. While fighting for a red flag those who attended the meeting came into conflict with the police and, as a result, many of them were arrested. Later, a poem in praise of the French Revolution and the execution of Louis XVI was found in the house of detention. The Japanese government considered this an insult to the emperor and the writer of the poem was charged with lese-majesty and sentenced to a three-year term of forced labour.

13. PREVALENCE OF ASSASSINATION

After the failure of the Russian Revolution of 1905 many Russian anarchists fled to Japan. The Chinese revolutionaries then resident in Japan were influenced by the ideas of these anarchists and also learned from them the method of carrying out terrorist activities, especially that of making bombs. Thus, simultaneously with the launching of uprisings, the practice of planning the assassination of Ching officials became very common. Assassination in the cause of chivalry was always considered noble in ancient China. In his revolutionary activities Dr. Sun Yat-sen also considered assassination an important revolutionary method. After 1905 the work of planning assassination became very important and the Revolutionary League set up a special department to take charge of that work. It was headed by Fang Chun-ying, a woman member of the league, but other members, including Huang Fu-sheng, Yu Yun-chi and myself, also helped. Our favourite reading material at that time was adventure novels and we frequently used them when studying methods of assassination.

Among the people active in planning assassinations Yu Yun-chi, a Szechuanese, was a hero especially worthy of commendation. Yu was a bit of a dandy when he first came to Japan and entered the Chiba Medical School. He was more interested in music and photography than in revolution. In the summer of 1908 he lived in the office of the *Szechuan Magazine* together with my eldest brother. After the failure of the Hokou Uprising in Yunnan his younger brother Yu Hua-wei contracted malignant malaria in Kanya, Yunnan. Later he went to Singapore for medical treatment and was in urgent need of money. Having received a letter from Yu Hua-wei soliciting my help, I collected 300 yen in a couple of days from the Szechuanese comrades and sent it to him post-haste. Yu Yun-chi was greatly affected by this, and recognizing the revolution as a noble cause where the comrades engaged in the work of revolution were as close to each other as brothers, he also wanted to join the Revolutionary League. He became a member upon my recommendation. After he had joined I explained to him that a revolutionary must give his all to the cause of revolution. He took my advice to heart, abandoned his extravagance and began to live in a simple way, becoming an entirely new man. He was very clever and mastered every kind of art quickly. He could take a watch or clock apart and reassemble it easily. And as he knew something about chemistry he gave us a great deal of help in making bombs. In the autumn of 1908 I returned to my school. Yu and my eldest brother rented another house where they devoted all their time to experimental work on explosives. One day, while they were working with two bottles of chemicals an explosion occurred, in which Yu was slightly injured. When a policeman arrived to see what had happened Yu pretended that he had been doing some research work and succeeded in hoodwinking the policeman. He continued his research until finally he made a powerful bomb. An improvement of the ignition mechanism guaranteed that there was absolutely no danger of explosion if the bomb was stored carefully. It was skilfully disguised, looked like a package of sweets and could be carried around without danger of detection.

By 1909 many armed uprisings launched by the Revolutionary League had failed and, in desperation, its members wanted to assassinate the Ching officials to avenge themselves. The most deeply hated of the Ching officials were Tuan Fang, governor-general of Kiangsu, Anhwei and Kiangsi, whose duty it was to defend the Yangtse estuary, and Li Chun, an admiral in charge of the defence of the Pearl River estuary. In the summer of 1909 Tuan Fang was transferred to the post of Minister of Trade for the Northern Ports. The Tientsin-Pukow Railway was not then built and the best way of travelling from Kiangsu to Peking was to sail by boat to Hankow and then travel by train on the Peking-Hankow Railway. We calculated that Tuan Fang would probably pass through Hankow when going north to assume his new post. We decided to send Yu Yun-chi and some other comrades to Hankow to make investigations and arrangements while we in Japan would help to raise funds and buy the materials. Yu went to Hankow and personally surveyed the topography. He made a detailed plan regarding where to plant the mine, where to hide and how to set off the mine. When he sent a chart of the detailed plan to us, we were very glad and sent him all the required materials. Everything was ready for the arch-criminal Tuan Fang to come into the death-trap set for him. Tuan Fang, however, was very wily and he pretended to go to Peking via Hankow, but when he arrived in Chenkiang he made a stop, saying that he would like to visit the beauty spot of Chiaoshan. As a matter of fact he secretly returned to Shanghai, and boarded an ocean liner for the north. Thus all our plans were made in vain.

Later, Wang Ching-wei suggested the assassination of Li Chun. Wang was a sort of effeminate scholar lacking in physical strength and with no knowledge of explosives. He wanted to carry out the assassination, because he had lost confidence in revolution and sought overnight fame by staking everything on a single throw. When he was in Hongkong he wrote twice to me asking for bombs. I sent him some, but when he received them he wavered and lacked courage to use them.

When Yu Yun-chi, Wang Ching-wei and others returned to Japan, we held a discussion and decided to pool all our resources and assassinate Tsai Feng, the prince regent who wielded the greatest power in the Ching government. In accordance with our decision, Yu Yun-chi and Huang Fu-sheng went to Peking in the autumn of 1909 to set up a secret organization. I stayed in Japan to make preparations. When Yu and Huang arrived in Peking they set up a secret organization in Liulichang Street under the guise of a photographic work-room called the Shouchen Studio, and then returned to Japan for explosives. At this time Wang Ching-wei was in love with a girl named Chen Pi-chun and they frequently said that as soon as Yu Yun-chi and Huang Fu-sheng had everything ready, they would go together and assassinate the prince regent.

When commenting on Wang Ching-wei's part in the attempt to assassinate Tsai Feng, Dr. Sun Yat-sen stated that after the failure of the uprisings "Wang Ching-wei became pessimistic and so he invited some comrades to go with him to Peking to make a desperate attempt on the life of the barbarian ruler". Dr. Sun Yat-sen was right in his analysis of Wang Ching-wei's motive. Indeed, Wang staked his life on the attempt because he was pessimistic, and not because of nobility of spirit, or the wish to fight for a worthy cause. Unfortunately Dr. Sun Yat-sen did not know all the facts regarding the planned attempt, so he thought that it was Wang Ching-wei who "invited some comrades" with him to Peking. As a matter of fact the honour of planning the attempt should go to Yu Yun-chi and Huang Fu-sheng. Wang Ching-wei and Chen Pi-chun joined in the attempt only at a later stage. Besides, Wang Ching-wei never did much of anything. To return to Yu Yun-chi and Huang Fu-sheng in Peking, they began by looking for an iron vessel and found one the size of a water-melon. They took it to an iron works and had it made into a bomb shell, filled it with the explosive which they had brought from Japan and made an exceedingly powerful bomb. The prince regent lived at a place northwest of Shihchahai Lake. Near his residence was a ditch spanned by a stone bridge and close by was a pit. The space below the bridge was an ideal one in which to plant the bomb. The pit could be used as a hide-out while the electric wire for setting off the bomb could be laid in the ditch. If the prince regent passed over the bridge the man hiding in the pit would pull the wire, the regent would be killed by the explosion, and the man would have a chance to escape. One April night in 1910 Yu and Huang went to the bridge, planted the bomb and then began to install the wire, but to their dismay, owing to an error in calculation, the wire was several feet short. This meant taking everything back and returning another time. While gathering their things, they heard someone relieving himself near the bridge, and had to step aside and wait a while. Just at that moment the gate of the regent's residence opened and some men came out with lanterns. Afraid of being discovered Yu and Huang left the bomb and fled. They returned the next night to take away the bomb but found that it was gone! After thinking the matter over they reached the conclusion that if the bomb had been taken away by the enemy it would be headline news the next day. If nothing was stirred up it could be assumed that the bomb had probably been taken away by someone living nearby. Several days passed quietly, and thinking that the danger was over, they sent Yu Yun-chi and Chen Pi-chun to Japan to get some more explosives for a second attempt. When Yu and Chen had arrived in Japan Chen stayed in Kobe and Yu came to see me. One day, while I was going to get the necessary materials for Yu I suddenly saw a news item in the paper saying that Huang Fu-sheng and Wang Ching-wei had been arrested. The regent had been very crafty. When the bomb was discovered he kept the matter quiet, but had it taken to a foreign embassy and carefully examined by a specialist. The specialist declared: "The explosive is very powerful. Since it requires a high degree of technical skill the bomb could not have been made in China, but the shell, which bears the mark of rough lathing, must be of local make." Acting on this clue the Ching government succeeded in locating the iron works where the shell had been made. Spies were then sent together with the manager of the iron works to comb the city to identify the man who called for the shell. They succeeded in identifying Huang Fu-sheng somewhere near Liulichang Street and also discovered the Shouchen

Studio. Pretending they wanted to have their pictures taken the spies went into the Shouchen Studio and arrested Huang Fu-sheng and all the personnel of the studio. Then, led by a man who used to bring meals for Wang Ching-wei, they succeeded in arresting Wang too.

In those days we were seething with enthusiasm and willing to sacrifice our lives to mete out punishment to the muddle-headed and cruel Ching officials, but we did not realize that the assassination of individual members of the ruling class could not overthrow the political rule of that class, much less could it shake its social foundation. This can only be understood when a Marxist outlook on history has been acquired.

14. THE CANTON UPRISING OF APRIL 27, 1911

After the arrest of Huang Fu-sheng and Wang Ching-wei the Ching government realized that revolution could not be prevented by the simple method of suppression. The men under arrest were not killed right away but were put in jail, to be slowly coaxed into submission. In the summer of 1910, in an attempt to get Huang Fu-sheng and Wang Ching-wei out of prison I went to Peking (via Korea) where I lodged in the house of my brother-in-law. For more than a month I tried to devise some way of getting them out. We had previously thought of breaking open the jail, but conditions at that time made this impossible. My brother-in-law knew that I had joined the revolutionaries, and suspecting that I was up to something, he bought a railway ticket for me, put me aboard the train by a trick and sent me to Shanghai.

In Shanghai I met Hsiung Keh-wu (Hsiung came to Shanghai after the failure of the Kuangan uprising of 1909 in Szechuan). Together we went to Hongkong to see Huang Hsing and plan the launching of an uprising in Canton.

Dr. Sun Yat-sen and Huang Hsing had previously agreed to launch a big uprising in Kwangtung. The Revolutionary League set up a headquarters in Hongkong from which to plan the uprising, making Huang Hsing responsible for the work. The uprising was to be launched on a very large scale. In addition to the preparations made in Kwangtung, people were sent to Kwangsi and to various provinces in the Yangtse valley to rally the people. The league members in Japan and Southeast Asia were also called on to take part. Previous uprisings had been planned in a desultory manner and had all failed. This time the uprising was planned with an all-out effort. It was to be a decisive battle to be fought to the bitter end. From this it can be seen that the uprising was still in the nature of military adventure and was not an act which could ensure success. Because of failures in previous uprisings, the preparations for this one was made with much more care and with much greater effort. Dr. Sun Yat-sen personally went to raise funds among the overseas Chinese, and procured about 200,000 dollars. In order to accumulate munitions, several groups of people were sent to foreign countries to purchase arms. As soon as I arrived in Hongkong I too was sent to Japan to buy munitions. Meanwhile Yu Yun-chi set up a secret establishment for the manufacture of bombs. A "dare-to-die" corps of 500 members was organized. This force later increased to 800. More than thirty secret centres were set up to help launch the uprising. The comrades from Szechuan used my name to set up an office known as "Old Man Wu's Residence". Later, after the uprising had failed a rumour went round saying that "Old Man Wu" had been killed, thus making me out to be a martyr. As a matter of fact I had never been in the "residence" because I had gone to Japan to buy fire-arms.

Although it was no easy matter to buy fire-arms, especially in quantities, it was still more difficult to sent them secretly to Hongkong and Canton. I remember that the first batch of munitions I bought consisted of 115 pistols and 4,000 rounds of cartridges. The man to whom I entrusted the delivery later proved to be a coward. Hearing that the munitions might be discovered by the customs officials in Hongkong, he threw them into the sea. Another batch of munitions in transit from Hongkong to Canton was lost through betrayal by a traitor. We set up "Hair Companies" in Hongkong and Canton and used the transport of hair as a cover for the shipping of munitions. Sometimes women comrades disguised themselves as brides and their bridal chairs were used to conceal the fire-arms. In short, the transport of munitions was a most difficult and dangerous job and we had to rack our brains to find all kinds of devices to conceal them.

On April 8, 1911, a member of the Revolutionary League in Canton named Wen Sheng-tsai, acting independently, assassinated Fu Chi, the garrison commander of Canton. This put Chang Ming-chi, Li Chun and other leading reactionary Ching officials in Canton on the alert. Coupled with the difficulty of transporting munitions this led to the postponement of the Canton Uprising from April 13 to April 27.

The Canton Uprising was finally launched at 5:30 p.m. on April 27 by a column of men led by Huang Hsing, who attacked the yamen of the governor-general. When they entered the inner court they found that Chang Ming-chi, the governor-general, had fled. Leaving the building they encountered a big contingent of enemy troops. Lin Shih-shuang, one of the revolutionaries, thinking that there might be revolutionaries among the enemy troops, wanted to tell them about the righteous cause of the revolution, but as soon as he shouted a few words he was killed by a shot. Huang Hsing was also hit by a shot which broke two of his fingers, but he continued to lead his men in the fight against the enemy. He fought as he retreated until he was the only man left. He then dived into a small shop, changed his clothes and fled to the home of a friend. That same night Yu Yun-chi and others led another column of men and attacked the yamen of the governor-general from the rear. Yu Yun-chi carried a basketful of bombs, led the men, throwing bombs as he went forward, and terrorized the enemy. However, as the revolutionaries were greatly outnumbered, Yu was wounded in many places and, after his bombs were all used up, he was taken captive. At the trial he declared heroically, "You can never kill a doctrine, much less a revolution." He died a martyr.

The uprising of April 27 continued until the next day. In this uprising the revolutionaries showed a spirit of incomparable heroism. For instance, Lin Chueh-min, who suffered martyrdom with great equanimity, wrote a touching letter to his wife before the uprising. During his trial he also wrote a deposition showing his resolute and unyielding spirit. It was written with tears and his life's blood. Still powerfully moving when read today these writings are worthy of being handed down to future generations. Li Wen-fu from Kwangtung and the many comrades from Huahsien County in the same province used sacks of rice in a grain shop as a breastwork as they fought the enemy until their death. The spirit shown by other martyrs was no less heroic.

Many revolutionaries died in this uprising. Later, when people came to collect the bodies of the martyrs for burial, seventy-two were found. To commemorate them the people of Canton buried them in a communal grave at Huanghuakang. Since then the "Seventy-two Martyrs of Huanghuakang" have become honoured throughout China.

Despite the martyrs' unmatched heroism, an armed revolt without the participation of the broad masses of people could not escape failure. This was the basic reason why the Canton Uprising did not succeed. There were other reasons too. The difficulty in transporting munitions, the presence of traitors among the revolutionaries and the fact that there were deserters were all important factors. But although the Canton Uprising failed and exceedingly great sacrifices were made, the blood of the martyrs was not shed in vain. Countless numbers of people were encouraged to carry on the revolutionary struggle and members of the reactionary ruling class became terrified. It was no accident that the tide of the 1911 Revolution came close in the wake of the Canton Uprising which certainly has a place in Chinese history especially that of the old-democratic revolution in China.

15. THE RAILWAY AGITATION

After the broad masses of people had carried out the struggle for several years for the right to open mines and build railways, the Ching government allowed the Szechuan-Hankow and Canton-Hankow Railways to be built by local private investments. But although the money to build these railways came from the people, the control of the railway companies was in the hands of the gentry and merchants, that is, the landlords and bourgeoisie, who were as corrupt as the officials of the Ching government. Owing to embezzlement and waste most of the railway funds were soon spent, and the work of building the railways made little progress. This situation caused great dissatisfaction among the people. They were dissatisfied with the gentry and merchants for monopolizing the work of railway construction and were still more resentful of the Ching government for selling the right to build railways to foreigners. At the beginning of 1911 the Ching government signed the contract for a loan with the Four-Power Consortium organized by Britain, the United States, France and Germany. Sheng Hsuan-huai, Minister of Communications, proposed that the government use the loan as a capital fund to carry out the nationalization of the railways to be built by the people of various provinces. On May 9 the Ching government issued a decree saying that all trunk railway lines would be nationalized and that this was to be a national policy. To intimidate the people it stated: "If anyone should disregard the public interest, purposely make

106

The monument erected in Szechuan after the Revolution of 1911 to commemorate the martyrs who died in the struggle to protect the railway rights. Beginning from May 1911, on the eve of the revolution, the people of Szechuan launched a movement to oppose the Ching government selling out the railway rights. The movement gave rise to a revolutionary tide which swept the whole province

The Tomb of the Seventy-two Martyrs in Huanghuakang, Canton. On April 27, 1911, under the leadership of Sun Yat-sen the China Revolutionary League launched the Canton Uprising, also known as the Huanghuakang Campaign, which failed owing to the lack of mass participation and insufficient preparations. However, it did exert a great influence on and give inspiration to the people of the whole country. The Canton Uprising was in fact a prelude to the Wuchang Uprising trouble for the railway administration and incite resistance he will be dealt with by law." The so-called nationalization of railways carried out by the Ching government meant selling the right to build railways to foreigners so that the court officials and the bureaucrat-compradors could make profit through the various transactions. On May 18 the Ching government appointed Tuan Fang director-general in charge of building the Canton-Hankow and Szechuan-Hankow Railways. He was ordered to take over the railway companies in Hunan, Hupeh, Kwangtung and Szechuan by force. On May 20 a contract was signed with Britain, the United States, France and Germany for the building of the Canton-Hankow Railway in Hunan and Hupeh Provinces and for the building of the Szechuan-Hankow Railway in Hupeh Province. Thus the right to build these railways, which had long ago been granted to the merchants and other people, was sold to the imperialists. This piratical and traitorous act of the Ching government was immediately opposed by the people of all social strata in Hunan, Hupeh, Kwangtung and Szechuan.

In an attempt to deceive the people and retard the progress of the revolutionary struggle, the Ching government had previously set up the State Assembly in Peking and the provincial assemblies. The greater part of the members in the provincial assemblies were from the gentry and upper bourgeoisie who favoured a constitutional monarchy. But as the Ching government's policy to nationalize the railways was a direct encroachment on their interests, they used the provincial assemblies, which were something like bourgeois parliamentary bodies, to launch a struggle for the protection of railway rights.

The first to rise in opposition to the government were the gentry and merchants in Hunan Province. They held meetings in the hall of the provincial assembly and distributed handbills, attacking the Ching government for accepting loans from foreign countries to build railways and thus giving away the nation's sovereign rights. The students added to the intensity of the struggle by holding protest strikes. Yang Wen-ting, governor of Hunan, realizing that the people were becoming furious, and fearing that the matter might lead to greater trouble, sent a memorial to the court asking for a return to the old policy. The government, however, severely reprimanded him and ordered him to suppress the people's struggle.

The struggle of the Hupeh people was still more vehement. Chan Ta-pei, a revolutionary, wrote an article entitled, "A Great Upheaval Is the Only Way to Save China", in which he advocated revolutionary measures. The article was carried by the *Ta Chiang Pao* (*Great River News*). Jui Cheng, governor-general of Hupeh and Hunan, had Chan Ta-pei arrested and the *Great River News* outlawed. People of various circles, numbering several thousand, held a meeting in the hall of the provincial assembly, during which one man wept bitterly and, shouting "Save the country", cut off one of his fingers. Representatives were chosen to go to Peking to petition the government. They went on hunger strike for three days in order to demonstrate their determination to carry on the struggle.

In Kwangtung, the shareholders of the Canton-Hankow Railway Company held a meeting unanimously expressing their opposition to the nationalization of railways. Chang Ming-chi, the governor-general of Kwangtung and Kwangsi, issued a notice nullifying the decisions made at this meeting. This made the people of Kwangtung still more indignant. They rushed to the government bank to cash their banknotes as a sign of protest. But under strong pressure from the reactionary government, the shareholders were forced to flee to Hongkong, where they organized an association for the protection of railway rights to continue their struggle. The *Chung Kuo Jih Pao* (*China Daily News*) published by the Revolutionary League and other newspapers strongly supported their struggle and Chang Ming-chi was so frightened that he issued a notice forbidding the distribution of Hongkong papers.

The Szechuan people's struggle to protect railway rights was even more vigorous and widespread. When the decree to nationalize the railways was issued in Szechuan the people were very indignant. In the middle of June a meeting was held in Chengtu by the representatives of the shareholders of the Szechuan-Hankow Railway Company. It was a very exciting meeting, many people wept and all were indignant. They cursed Sheng Hsuan-huai and called him a traitor. They declared that the Ministry of Communications was an office for selling out the country. The meeting decided to organize an association for the protection of railway rights, and elected Pu Tien-chun and Lo Lun to be president and vice-president respectively. Representatives were sent to carry out propaganda in all parts of the province. Associations for the protection of railway rights were established in various counties. The movement grew, spreading throughout the whole province. Towards the end of August the merchants and students of Chengtu staged strikes, and by the beginning of September the movement had reached such a height that the people refused to pay taxes and duties. Fearing that the movement might even go so far as to destroy the feudal order, the constitutional monarchists tried to keep it within limits. A notice was put out by Pu Tien-chun and others, asking the people to limit their struggle to the question of railway rights, and not to oppose the government and especially not to stage revolts. A revolutionary struggle waged by the broad masses of people, however, could not be controlled by a handful of constitutional monarchists, especially when there were revolutionaries pushing it forward. Although the movement was to a large extent spontaneous and not entirely led by the Revolutionary League, certain members of the league like Lung Ming-chien and Wang Tien-chieh did play a fairly important role in the movement and gave some impetus to its development. Lung, Wang and I all came from the province of Szechuan. Lung was a returned student from Japan, and had taken part in the 1908 Hokou Uprising in Yunnan Province, where he continued to work for some time after its failure. Later he came back to Szechuan and was elected a member of the provincial assembly. He also ran a law school in Chengtu. He carried on revolutionary work by taking advantage of these conditions. These members of the league had seen through the real character of Pu Tien-chun and other constitutional monarchists from the very beginning of the movement. They knew that the constitutional monarchists did not dare to go against the reactionary rule of the Ching government. So, in addition to co-operating with the constitutional monarchists in a legal struggle, they secretly contacted the secret societies to prepare for armed uprisings. At the beginning of August 1911 Lung Ming-chien and Wang Tien-chieh held a meeting in Tzechow with the leaders of the Society of Brothers, one of the major secret societies in Szechuan. In accordance with the policy of engaging in both open and secret struggles proposed by Lung Ming-chien, they decided to organize an "Army of Comrades" to prepare for armed revolt. Lung Ming-chien arrived in the city when the merchants and students of Chengtu were about to hold strikes. To quickly spread the struggle in order to win the support of the people of the whole province, he and other comrades prepared several hundred wooden boards on which were written the following words: "Struggle now on in Chengtu. Quick response from all places is expected." The boards were varnished with wood-oil, wrapped in oil-paper and thrown into the river. Later these boards were commonly referred to by the people as "water telegrams". These "water telegrams" floated down the river. When the people living in the lower reaches learned that the struggle had begun in the provincial capital they all responded. On September 9 Chao Erh-feng, governor-general of Szechuan, played a trick on Pu Tien-chun, Lo Lun and others. He told them to come to his yamen because good news had come from Peking. As soon as they arrived he had them arrested. He also had the railway company closed. This enraged the Chengtu people and tens of thousands of them went to the yamen of the governor-general, demanding the release of the arrested. Chao Erh-feng ordered his men to open fire. Dozens of people were killed and a countless number were wounded. However, the people did not yield to Chao's frantic suppression; on the contrary, they intensified and extended their struggle. The entire province of Szechuan was soon boiling over and a great uprising, involving the people of the whole province, broke out. Besieged by the "Army of Comrades" from various counties Chao Erh-feng, hitherto so arrogant and brutish, now found himself helpless in Chengtu. The Ching government was frightened and frantic. It hastily ordered Tuan Fang, who had previously been sent to Wuhan[1] to take over the Canton-Hankow and Szechuan-Hankow Railway Companies, to go to Szechuan with a contingent of the new army of Hupeh and carry out suppressive measures. This fanned the flames of this struggle, making the people of Szechuan even more angry. Meanwhile the dispatch of the Hupeh army to the west weakened the defensive power of Wuhan, and gave the revolutionaries of the triple cities an opportunity to launch an uprising. It created exceedingly favourable conditions for the subsequent Wuchang Uprising and in a large measure accounted for its success.

16. JUNGHSIEN BECOMES INDEPENDENT

After the failure of the Canton Uprising in April 1911 some comrades and myself hastily left for Japan. Shortly after my arrival the railway agitation started. Believing that the revolutionary movement would continue to develop I decided to return to China and take part in it. I arrived in Shanghai in June. At this time in Shanghai a number of league members, led by Sung Chiao-jen, were organizing the Central China Headquarters of the Revolutionary League. Nominally

---

[1] The triple cities of Wuchang, Hankow and Hanyang.

a branch of the Revolutionary League it was really meant to be an independent organization. With the Yangtse valley as a centre, it aimed to agitate for revolution in the central part of China, and opposed any attempt to continue the launching of uprisings in the frontier regions. In this it was correct. Widespread riots were in progress among the hungry masses who attacked the rice-hoarders and refused to pay taxes. These riots were most frequent in the Yangtse River valley and Shantung. In the spring of 1910 more than 20,000 hungry people were involved in a large-scale rice riot in Changsha. They seized grain, burned the yamen of the governor and the foreign churches. In the summer of the same year tens of thousands of people in Laiyang, Shantung, rose against the payment of special taxes. In 1911 when the Yangtse valley was plagued by big floods, riots of hungry people and struggles against the levying of special taxes became much more widespread. Rice riots in Liuyang, Hunan, and in Hangchow and Ningpo, Chekiang, were waged on a large scale. Meanwhile the workers in Shanghai, Hankow and other cities were becoming increasingly active in waging struggles, in addition to the railway agitation. All this swelled the revolutionary tide. It is true that the Central China Headquarters of the Revolutionary League did not realize the direction in which the revolutionary movement was moving, but its call for action conformed to the actual conditions. I did not stay in Shanghai very long nor did I see Sung Chiao-jen. Sung and his colleagues had made me responsible for the work of the Revolutionary League in Szechuan, but this was done without my knowledge. From Shanghai I went to Ichang. On my way I saw that the people were exceedingly dissatisfied with the Ching government and that they sympathized with the revolution. In Ichang I saw the workers and other employees of the Szechuan-Hankow Railway carrying out activities to protect the railway. I had the feeling that something unusual was about to happen. From Ichang I sailed upstream on *S.S. Shutung* which plied the

Yangtse River in Szechuan. Although it was only a steam tug with a trailer in tow, the *Shutung* was much faster and safer than the junk which we used to sail when we left Szechuan before. But even such a simple vessel was under the control of foreigners. Its technical personnel were foreigners and even the captain was a foreigner. The ferocious captain, with the air of an imperialist, treated the Chinese people brutally. As the weather was hot and the trailer was crowded, many passengers went to sleep at night on an open boat which they had tied to the trailer. The next morning, as soon as the steam tug whistled, the crew cut the ropes tying the boat to the trailer and set sail without letting the passengers come aboard. When the passengers in the boat awoke they realized that the steamship had gone. They were in a dreadful fix and did not know what to do, as the steamship was travelling very quickly, the waves were swelling, and the boat was in danger of overturning. They shouted for help. I could not tolerate this and urged the other passengers in the trailer to hold a meeting in the dining-room. All the passengers were extremely angry and cursed the foreigners for being unreasonable and heedless of the fate of the Chinese passengers. When the foreign captain heard the passengers cursing him he threatened them with a pistol. The passengers were not afraid of him; on the contrary they became more angry and cursed still more vehemently. Seeing that the situation was getting out of hand, the comprador aboard the ship persuaded the captain to return to his cabin and had the passengers in the boat brought back to the trailer. The comprador was overheard telling the captain: "These people are returned students and nobody dares to provoke them." I thought to myself, "Ah! Ah! So you're afraid of returned students, then I'll show you the real strength of the Chinese people!" I continued to address the passengers on the necessity of saving the country. The situation became tense and there was again a great uproar. Frightened, the foreigners and the comprador kept silent and dared not provoke the passengers again.

I returned to Junghsien, my home county, before Chinese All Souls' Day (fifteenth day of the seventh moon in the lunar calendar). One day I went to the county town; as I was approaching the south gate of the city I saw a man at the head of some troops marching towards me. Entering the city I went up to the man and saw that he was Lung Ming-chien. I learned that immediately after sending out the "water telegrams" to encourage uprisings he had gone back to Junghsien. There he had joined the uprising launched by Wang Tien-chieh and others, organized an armed force, and was now leading his men in an attack on Chengtu. He was very glad to see me and said, "It's mighty good that you've come back. The Association for the Protection of the Railway Rights is led by Pu Tien-chun, Lo Lun and other constitutional monarchists and nothing good can be expected from them. We must organize more armed forces and lead the people to rise in struggle if a way out is to be found. I'm now going to the front. I hope you will make plans for all the things that are to be done." Saying this he and Wang Tien-chieh led more than 1,000 men off to Chengtu. Going out of the city Lung became very excited, and declared, "I will not enter this gate again if I don't kill Chao Erh-feng." His men were all very moved by his declaration.

On their way to Chengtu, Lung Ming-chien and Wang Tien-chieh met Ching troops in the vicinity of Jenshou and a battle ensued. Later, their men were merged with the troops under Chin Tsai-keng, leader of the Society of Brothers, who had joined the uprising. The Eastern Army command was then formed with Chin Tsai-keng and Wang Tien-chieh as commander and deputy commander, and Lung Ming-chien as chief-of-staff. The Eastern Army fought against Ching troops in the regions around Jenshou and Chengtu, but owing to inferior equipment and lack of reinforcements it was defeated in a battle at Chinhuangsze. Wang Tien-chieh and Lung Ming-chien led a detachment to attack Chiating and then Hsufu. Lung Ming-chien, fatigued after his unsuccessful military operations, fell sick during the march. He became worse and died in a village near Yipin, his aim still unrealized. Lung Ming-chien had fought for the Chinese bourgeois democratic revolution all his life and played a great role especially in the movement to protect the railway rights. He used the right tactics to push forward the development of the revolutionary movement, and when the time was ripe he unhesitatingly launched an armed struggle. During the critical period in the summer of 1911, despite the intense heat he went back and forth between Junghsien and Chengtu six or seven times. His indefatigable spirit and the manner in which he carried out his tasks for the cause of revolution are worthy of our respect. Overwork was the cause of his ill health and he finally sacrificed his life for the revolutionary cause. On his death-bed he still thought of the revolution and made many important suggestions to Wang Tien-chieh. Although he died far from his home his funeral was attended by 13,000 people, a tribute of their love for him. Men like Lung Ming-chien were the real heroes of the Revolution of 1911. In the past bourgeois historians have seldom mentioned his name. The real creators and judges of history, however, are the people and since they loved him so much his name will never die in spite of all the distortions and evasions of bourgeois historians.

After Lung Ming-chien and Wang Tien-chieh had left Junghsien with the men, I had the entire responsibility for work in the rear. I had to carry out a struggle against the local officials and landed gentry and at the same time raise funds for the comrades' military expenses. As soon as I made some headway in fund-raising I stepped up the training of militiamen in a number of villages. I also opened a military training class so that the army fighting in the front could be continuously reinforced and expanded.

After Lung Ming-chien had left the army because of serious illness Wang Tien-chieh led the men back to Junghsien. Upon hearing that Wang Tien-chieh had returned to the county, the magistrate of Junghsien, appointed by the Ching government, and Kuo Sheng-chih, as well as other local despots all ran away. Wang Tien-chieh discussed with me what should be done next. I suggested that Junghsien be declared independent and that we run the government of the county ourselves. All the comrades agreed. On September 25, Wang Tien-chieh and I called a rally of people of all circles in the county town. I made a speech and declared Junghsien independent. The Revolutionary Government of Junghsien was announced amidst thunderous cheers. This established a base for the Eastern Army.

The uprising of Junghsien had been launched in early August 1911, two months ahead of that in Wuchang. The independence of Junghsien was declared on September 25, two weeks earlier than the Wuchang Uprising. Its influence was therefore very great and Junghsien soon became the centre of the anti-Ching armed struggle southeast of Chengtu. At the time Junghsien was declared independent the armed uprising covered more than ten cities including Pengshan, Meichow, Hungya and Chiakiang. Unfortunately the occupation forces were never able to consolidate their position and these places were captured and lost in quick succession. Junghsien was the only place where a revolutionary government remained.

Although Junghsien was based on a firm footing the revolutionary government of a small county could hardly be expected to exist by itself. We had to expand and we launched an attack on Weiyuan which was easily taken. Then we launched another on Tzeliuching, were resisted by a large number of garrison troops and the result was a stalemate. By this time the Wuchang Uprising had broken out, but owing to the enemy blockade we were unable to learn either quickly or clearly what was happening outside the county.

We heard rumours that a "rebellion" of the revolutionaries had occurred in Hupeh and that a man by the name of Li had become the military governor. We were puzzled because we thought that if an uprising had been launched by the revolutionaries, it should have been done under the banner of Dr. Sun Yat-sen and we wondered what this man Li had to do with it. As our effort was confined to a local struggle and we had no means of knowing the general situation in the country, we were very much worried and felt a great need to get in touch with the outside world.

17. THE WUCHANG UPRISING

However, the rumours proved to be true, for the so-called "rebellion" in Hupeh was the Wuchang Uprising on October 10, and Li, who had become the military governor, was no other than Li Yuan-hung, former brigade commander of the new army in Hupeh.

The Wuchang Uprising was not something that just happened. It was the result of the developing revolutionary situation in the whole country. The agitation concerning the railway and the popular armed uprisings in Szechuan were the essential factors leading to the outbreak of the uprising. It was also the result of the many years of hard work by the revolutionaries in Hunan and Hupeh, and the efficient activities of the revolutionaries in the new army were the primary factors in the success of the Wuchang Uprising.

Revolutionary groups were already organized in Wuhan in 1904 and agitational and organizational work had been consistently carried out among the soldiers. Before the 1911 Revolution there were two revolutionary organizations in Wuhan, the Literary Association and the Society for Mutual Progress. The Literary Association used literature as a front behind which they carried out intensive activities among the soldiers of the new army for the purpose of expanding revolutionary organizations. It published a newspaper called *Ta Chiang Pao* (*Great River News*) which carried revolutionary propaganda. The leading members of the association were Chiang Yi-wu, Chan Ta-pei, Yang-wang Peng, Liu Fu-chi and Li Liu-ju and by July 1911 its membership exceeded 5,000. The total number of men in the new army of Hupeh was only about 16,000 and nearly a third of them belonged to the Literary Association. This shows that with the unfolding of the revolutionary movement, thanks to the work of the revolutionaries, the new army, the main prop of the reactionary Ching government, had gradually become revolutionary in outlook. The Society for Mutual Progress was organized in Japan in 1907 by the merging of various secret societies. It adopted the programme of the Revolutionary League (see Section 12). Later its leaders returned to China to engage in revolutionary activities, and the society became a fairly powerful organization in Hunan and Hupeh. In the summer of 1911, prompted by the Revolutionary League, and after many talks, the Society for Mutual Progress and the Literary Association, two revolutionary organizations with a comparatively broad popular basis, united. In August they realized that the railway agitation was leading to an uprising and that the time for revolution had come. They therefore established a joint command and prepared to launch a big uprising. The provisional headquarters of the uprising was at No. 85 Hsiao-chao Street, Wuchang, with Chiang Yi-wu, leader of the Literary Association, as commander-in-chief and Sun Wu, leader of the Society for Mutual Progress, as chief-of-staff.

Early in September, the reactionary Ching government, alarmed and frightened by the revolutionary struggle of the people in Szechuan, ordered the new army of Hupeh to send a contingent of men to Szechuan to suppress the revolutionary struggle there. Jui Cheng, governor-general of Hupeh and Hunan, knew that the new army was a hot-bed of revolutionaries, and was only too glad that some of its men were being sent away. The revolutionaries, however, feared that the splitting of the new army into two parts would hinder the revolution and made great haste to prepare for the launching of an uprising. They held a meeting on September 24 and decided to launch an uprising on October 6, the day of the Mid-Autumn Festival. Soon the story about the killing of the Tartars on the Mid-Autumn Festival[1] was circulating throughout Wuhan. The situation became more and more tense. Jui Cheng now realized that the dispatch of the troops had weakened the power of defence and created favourable conditions for the revolutionaries and untold difficulties for himself. Frightened, worried and constantly on tenterhooks, he made his temporary residence in a gunboat and secretly slept there every night.

Because the preparatory work was not satisfactorily done the time scheduled for the launching of the uprising had to be postponed ten days. On the morning of October 9, however, an accident occurred in a house in the Paoshanli Lane, in the Russian concession of Hankow. The revolutionaries were manufacturing bombs there and an explosion occurred, wounding Sun Wu in the head. The establishment was immediately raided and all banners, insignias, documents and seals were taken away by the police. The plan for the uprising was exposed and Chiang Yi-wu, fearing that postponement would cause further losses, issued an urgent order, in the name of the commander-in-chief, to launch the uprising at midnight that very day. Before the order could be transmitted to all the men concerned, the headquarters in Hsiaochao Street and many other centres were raided. A large number of the leading members of the uprising were arrested and Chiang Yi-wu had a narrow escape. That evening Jui Cheng cruelly murdered the arrested leaders of the uprising. At the same time he had the gates of the city and the

---

[1] This story refers to the people's revolt against the Mongol rulers at the end of the Yuan Dynasty.

entrances to the barracks closed and, making use of the captured list of names, he ordered a thorough search for all people connected with the uprising. The situation was very tense and the city was in great turmoil. The people were alarmed and did not know what to do. All kinds of rumours were in circulation. The revolutionaries knew that they were in great danger and all the people connected with them were worried too. They felt that to rise and fight was better than to wait for death.

On October 10 Jui Cheng ordered his men to continue hunting for the revolutionaries whose names were on the captured list. He also threatened that all the revolutionaries were to be killed. Terror reigned in the triple cities of Wuhan. The revolutionary members of the new army decided to resist and fight their way out. At seven o'clock in the evening Hsiung Ping-kun, Chin Chao-lung and other soldiers of the rear company, 8th Engineering Battalion, 8th Division of the new army in Wuchang, were about to revolt when their plans were discovered by Tao Chi-sheng, a platoon leader. Tao ordered his men to arrest Chin. Chin shouted "Revolt, comrades!" and the soldiers of the whole company responded at once. Some of the reactionary officers were killed and others fled when they learned of the uprising. More than forty soldiers had revolted, and under the leadership of Hsiung Ping-kun they marched to attack the arsenal at Chuwangtai. The soldiers of the Left Company of the 8th Engineering Battalion garrisoned at Chuwangtai also joined the uprising that same night and the Chuwangtai arsenal was occupied by the insurgent troops. When the revolutionaries in other parts of Wuchang heard the sound of firing they too joined in the uprising and rushed towards Chuwangtai. After some deliberations the leaders of the uprising decided to attack the yamen of the governor-general and kill Jui Cheng, but owing to the disorderliness of the troops and the lack of a unified command the attack was repulsed. Meanwhile the uprising spread wider and wider as an increasing number of soldiers joined, and Hsiung Ping-kun felt that the work of commanding was too difficult for him. Just at this time Wu Chao-lin, commander of the Left Company of the Engineering Battalion, who had run away when he saw the troops at Chuwangtai joining in the uprising, was brought back to Hsiung. As Wu had enjoyed some prestige among the soldiers he was made the provisional commander-in-chief of the uprising. He mapped out a plan for the attack, military discipline was strengthened and a new assault on the governor-general's yamen was launched. Jui Cheng, thoroughly alarmed, climbed over a wall and fled to a gunboat. The sound of firing also frightened other Ching officials who went into hiding one after the other. By the morning of the 11th, Wuchang was completely occupied by the insurgent troops.

In this way the first success was scored, but the question then arose as to who would assume leadership. Many of the former leaders of the uprising had been arrested and killed, others had fled, and the troops were left leaderless. Acting on a suggestion made by Wu Chao-lin they asked Li Yuan-hung, former brigade commander of the new army, to be military governor and Tang Hua-lung, speaker of the provincial assembly, to be minister of civil affairs. Tang Hua-lung was a well-known constitutional monarchist who had never sympathized with the revolution. Li Yuan-hung had previously murdered many revolutionaries and, on the very night of the uprising, he even killed a revolutionary soldier who was delivering a message to him. When he saw the uprising continuing in full blast he had taken refuge in the house of one of his secretaries. He trembled with fear when Wu Chao-lin sent a man to ask him to come out. He refused to support the uprising and even questioned Wu as to why he had rebelled. However, he was made military governor. He dared not sign the proclamation to the people and when the troops forcibly cut off his queue he wept for the loss of that vestige of enslavement. It was only on October 17 after the occupation of both Hankow and Hanyang and a declaration of "neutrality" by the foreign consulates in Hankow that Li Yuan-hung really took office as military governor. After the Wuchang Uprising, with men like Li Yuan-hung and Tang Hua-lung in the saddle, it was no wonder that the struggle gradually declined and took the path of compromise with the reactionary forces.

Following the victory of the Wuchang Uprising province after province declared itself independent. The reactionary rule of the Ching Dynasty, which had lasted more than two hundred years, soon collapsed. But conditions in these provinces were much the same as those in Wuhan. The fruits of revolution did not fall into the hands of the people. They were snatched away by the warlords, bureaucrats and constitutional monarchists.

18. THE NEIKIANG AND CHUNGKING UPRISINGS

In September 1911, having been ordered by the Ching government to "go to Szechuan to carry out investigation and suppression", Tuan Fang led a big contingent of the Hupeh army and marched proudly westwards, determined on annihilation. But before he and his men arrived in Chengtu the Wuchang Uprising had occurred. Tuan Fang entered Szechuan with great pomp, but the further he went the more he felt that he was encircled by the people. Frightened out of his wits by the news of the Wuchang Uprising, he stopped at Tzechow and did not dare to go on any further. He sent a detachment of troops to Tzeliuching to reinforce the garrison troops, who were besieged by the revolutionary forces. The men of this detachment stopped at the border between Neikiang and Weiyuan. The army formed at the time of the Junghsien Uprising had been besieging and attacking Tzeliuching for a long time. Knowing that there were revolutionaries in the Hupeh army, Wu Shu-hsien and I left Tzeliuching for Neikiang on November 21, to establish con-

The Military Government of Hupeh
established after the Wuchang Uprising

Dr. Sun Yat-sen (*fifth from left, front row*) at the presidential inauguration. On January 1, 1912, the Provisional Government of the Republic of China was established to elect Dr. Sun as Provisional President

nections with them. Two days later we made contact, and it was agreed that they would take immediate action to kill Tuan Fang, while we would proceed to launch an uprising in Neikiang where there were many revolutionaries.

On November 25 Tuan Fang's troops, true to their word, staged an uprising. Tuan Fang, who had been a veritable despot, humbly implored the soldiers to spare his life, saying that his ancestors were really people of Han nationality and that his family had only become Manchus four generations ago. He hoped this lie would save his life, but the soldiers had no pity for this shameless man who had committed many crimes, and executed him without any qualms. Chen Chen-fan was then elected commander of the Hupeh army in Szechuan, and he immediately sent a man to Neikiang to get in touch with me.

On November 26 we began to take action in Neikiang. The magistrate of that county fled at once upon hearing that Tuan Fang had been killed in Tzechow. The men of the garrison followed his example, thereby creating favourable conditions for us to easily dispose of the local forces. We convened a mass meeting that very day. It was attended by several thousand enthusiastic people. I addressed the meeting, announced the aim of the revolution and proposed to set up a revolutionary government. The people shouted, "Long live the revolution", their voices resounding again and again. A resolution was passed to set up a Neikiang military government. I was elected head of the administrative department and Wu Shu-hsien head of the military department. Thousands of people conducted us to the yamen of the former magistrate to take office. This gave me a deep sense of the power of the people. As an old saying goes, "To stand for them (that is, the people) is to be successful and to stand against them is to fail."

Because Tuan Fang had been killed in Tzechow and the Neikiang Uprising was successful the attack on Tzeliuching also ended in victory.

When we were launching the uprising in Neikiang we did not know that Chungking had also become independent on November 22. This was how it happened. On November 5 Hsia Chih-shih launched an uprising in Lungchuanyi near Chengtu. Hsia, who came from Hokiang, Szechuan, was a former student of the Tohin School in Japan, where he had joined the Revolutionary League. After graduation he returned to China and became a platoon leader of the Ching army stationed in Chengtu. When the movement to protect the railway rights had reached its climax he realized that the time for revolution had come and prepared to launch an uprising. At that time he was ordered to lead a detachment of infantry to the garrison in Lungchuanyi. He secretly carried out revolutionary propaganda among the soldiers who were greatly moved, and expressed their willingness to join the revolution. At that time there were an army service corps and a detachment of cavalry stationed in Lungchuanyi. Hsia sent some men to carry out revolutionary propaganda among them too, and the officers and men of these two units agreed to act in unison with Hsia's men. On the evening of November 5 Hsia mustered the men of the three units, numbering more than 200, in a temple near the garrison and then launched an uprising. The commander of the troops in Lungchuanyi was killed on the spot, and the men elected Hsia Chih-shih commander of the revolutionary army which immediately marched eastwards towards Chungking. As Tuan Fang's troops were then in Tzechow they made a detour through northern Szechuan. They were welcomed by the people all along the way, and many joined their ranks. Hsia and his men arrived on the outskirts of Chungking on November 21. The revolutionaries inside Chungking sent men to establish contact with them. The next day with their help Hsia and his men triumphantly entered Chungking. The reactionary Ching officials then realized that their power was at an end. All of them, with the exception of some who had already fled, were compelled to surrender. On that same day people of all

124

circles in Chungking held a big meeting in the Chaotienkuan temple. The Szechuan Military Government was set up. Chang Pei-chueh, a member of the Revolutionary League, was elected military governor and Hsia Chih-shih vice-military governor. Independence was announced through a public statement made to the people of the whole country.

The Szechuan Military Government repeatedly wrote and sent wires asking me to go to Chungking. I already knew that the Wuchang Uprising was successful and that it had met with response from all parts of the country. After thinking over the general situation, I reached the conclusion that before we could go ahead with our work, connections must be established with the central organization directing the revolution of the whole country. On the night of December 2, after having made arrangements for the work in Neikiang, I set out for Chungking. I did not stay there long, but left for Nanking. By this time the revolutionary forces had captured Nanking and plans were being made to establish a provisional government of the Chinese Republic in Nanking. Dr. Sun Yat-sen had returned from abroad and was on his way to the city. The Szechuan Military Government sent Yang Shu-kan and me to Nanking, as its representatives, to participate in the work of the provisional government.

19. THE CHENGTU COUPS

Immediately after its establishment the Chungking Military Government organized an army and made preparations for an attack on Chengtu. With the revolutionary tide sweeping over Szechuan and extending over the whole country, a number of coups took place in Chengtu. The success of the Tzechow and Neikiang uprisings and the attack on Tzeliuching had extended the influence and power of the revolutionary forces around Chengtu. Chao Erh-feng, the governor-general of Szechuan, had been besieged for several months. Realizing that reinforcements could not be expected and that the fall of Chengtu was only a matter of time, he thought that rather than be overthrown by the revolutionaries, it would be better for him to hand the government to the constitutional monarchists and thus preserve his own power. So on November 27, with the collaboration of Chao Erh-feng and the constitutional monarchists, a farce of "independence" was staged. The "Great Han Military Government of Szechuan" was established with Pu Tien-chun, head of the constitutional monarchists, as military governor and Chu Ching-lan, the right-hand man of Chao Erh-feng and commander of the new army, as vice-military governor. Chao Erh-feng was given an important post in frontier defence but, as a matter of fact, he still wielded de facto power both military and political. Needless to say the people were not satisfied with this kind of "independence". Under the slogan of "Catch Chao" the revolutionary forces continued to march towards Chengtu. Meanwhile Chao Erh-feng, knowing that the Ching government had not yet fallen, plotted a comeback. On December 8, when Pu Tien-chun was holding a military review, the garrison troops, urged on by Chao Erh-feng, mutinied. After that Pu Tien-chun fled into hiding and did not dare take the office of the military governor again. The revolutionary forces on the outskirts of the city were angry, stormed into the city and surrounded Chao Erh-feng's official residence. Thus Chao Erh-feng's hopes of staging a comeback failed. The military government reorganized itself in an attempt to hoodwink the people and pacify the revolutionary forces. Yin Chang-heng, a returned student from Japan and formerly the principal of the Military Academy, became the military governor, and Lo Lun, a constitutional monarchist who had connections with the Society of Brothers, was made vice-military governor. A few revolutionaries were given posts as departmental heads as a bit of window-dressing. The people's anger with regard to Chao Erh-feng, however, was not appeased. Fearing that this might lead to a revolution of a more radical nature and in an attempt to lull the people's anger, the constitutional monarchists were finally forced to kill Chao Erh-feng. On December 22, relying on the revolutionary forces, Yin Chang-heng and the constitutional monarchists disarmed the troops under the control of the governor-general and put an end to Chao Erh-feng. The constitutional monarchists then tried to take over the command of the revolutionary forces, employing both soft and tough tactics. Because the leaders of the revolutionary forces lacked a correct ideology, some were corrupted and bought over. Others were cruelly murdered. Thus the great revolutionary movement collapsed and the fruits of the people's hard struggle were seized by the constitutional monarchists.

From what has been said it can be seen that Chao Erh-feng was the most die-hard representative of the reactionary Ching rule in Szechuan. He left no stone unturned to save the Ching government in Szechuan from being overthrown. He was unswervingly loyal to it from beginning to end and his life ended with the overthrow of the reactionary rule of the Ching Dynasty. The constitutional monarchists, having Pu Tien-chun and Lo Lun as their leaders, represented the interests of the landlords and upper bourgeoisie of Szechuan. Although they had taken advantage of the power of the revolutionary masses to launch a limited struggle against the reactionary Ching rulers, they were afraid of the masses carrying out a revolution which would rock the social foundation of feudal rule. They were, therefore, always lenient towards the representatives of the reactionary Ching government such as Chao Erh-feng but exceptionally cruel towards the people who took part in the uprisings. The insurgent forces were largely composed of people of the lower social strata who spontaneously took part in the struggle. Most of their leaders were from the secret societies and only a few of them were revolutionaries. Among these leaders there were many men of noble character such as Lung Ming-chien, for instance. Unfortunately, most of them sacrificed their lives in these severe struggles. Those who remained fell into the traps set by the constitutional monarchists and inadvertently became their tools in the fight for political power. However, full credit must go to the people of the lower social strata, and their leaders, with regard to both the movement to protect the railway rights and to overthrow the Ching Dynasty. Chao Erh-feng was a butcher, most of the constitutional monarchists were swindlers, while the majority in the revolutionary forces were good people. This is no mere empty talk, but the historical judgement of the broad masses of people.

The situation in Szechuan at that time may be briefly described as follows: Chungking was in the hands of the revolutionaries while Chengtu was under the control of the constitutional monarchists. Chungking and Chengtu were thus two opposing camps.

20. THE PROVISIONAL GOVERNMENT OF NANKING

The Ching government was greatly alarmed by the Wuchang Uprising. It hastily sent Yin Chang, minister of war, with two regiments of the Northern Army to suppress the rising. The officers of the Northern Army, however, were all Yuan Shih-kai's henchmen and would not take orders from Yin Chang. At that time many influential persons among the foreign imperialists and the Chinese feudal ruling class were of the opinion that Yuan Shih-kai was a "great man" and that he was the only one who could save the Chinese reactionaries from their doom. Driven to its last resources the Ching government was forced to reinstate him in office. Previously, when trying to win the goodwill of the influential court officials, Yuan Shih-kai had found favour in the eyes of Jung Lu, a high-ranking official in the Ching government, and had been made provincial judge in Chihli Province. During the coup d'etat of 1898, when the reformers wanted to use his power to checkmate the die-hards, he informed Jung Lu, thus frustrating the reform movement. During the Yi Ho Tuan

Movement in 1900, when he was governor of Shantung Province, he ruthlessly persecuted the men taking part in this movement. Later he held the posts of the governor-general of Chihli and grand councillor, wielding great military and political power. In 1908 Tsai Feng, the prince regent, adopted an anti-Han policy and dismissed Yuan from office. Yuan went back to his own home in Changteh, Honan Province, for the sake of his "health", but in reality, he was still the leader of the Northern Army which grew under his care. When the revolution broke out and the Ching government was in danger of being overthrown he regarded this as a rare opportunity for political manoeuvring. The Ching government appointed him governor-general of Hupeh and Hunan but he refused to take office. It was only when the Ching government complied with all his demands, promising to invest him with full power and appoint him prime minister that he consented to make preparations for the fight against the revolutionaries.

After the Wuchang Uprising Chu Fei-huang, a Szechuan member of the Revolutionary League, realizing that Yuan Shih-kai was likely to become powerful, went to Changteh to try his fortune. Wearing cotton clothes and a straw hat, Yuan spent his time fishing all day long and pretended that he was no longer interested in national affairs. Chu advised Yuan to take over military and political power from the Ching government first and then cast his lot in with the revolutionaries, claiming that they would certainly agree to let him unify the country. Chu also offered his services to get in touch with the revolutionaries. Although Yuan did not openly express his opinion he was secretly pleased with Chu's idea, kept him as his advisor and treated him with great respect. Once he had obtained power from the Ching government Yuan, however, did not cast his lot in with the revolutionaries, but wanted the revolutionaries to serve him. He wanted to be the dictator of China. Before Yuan went to Peking to form a cabinet the Ching government had already been compelled, by circumstances, to release Wang Ching-wei and Huang Fu-sheng from prison where they had been put for attempting to assassinate Tsai Feng, the prince regent. After his release Wang Ching-wei organized the Revolutionary League of Peking and Tientsin with Li Shih-tseng and other representatives of the big bureaucrats, landlords and compradors of the north. Although there were true revolutionaries in this league its leading members were men like Wang Ching-wei and Li Shih-tseng who were trumpet blowers for Yuan Shih-kai. Like many Chinese and foreign reactionaries they considered that Yuan Shih-kai was the only man who could set things right in China. Wang Ching-wei became a sworn brother of Yuan Keh-ting, Yuan Shih-kai's eldest son, in order to court the favour of the father.

Having obtained power from the counter-revolutionaries and entered into collusion with the disreputable elements in the revolutionary camp, Yuan Shih-kai was able to manoeuvre between the revolution and counter-revolution, either in attacking or bargaining with the revolutionaries. After his cabinet was formed and the revolution began making rapid progress, Yuan decided on attack. He sent his men to assassinate Wu Lu-chen, commander of the 6th Division of the Ching army who being a revolutionary was planning to stage an uprising in Shihchiachuang. This consolidated Yuan's position in Peking and Chihli, the centre of the counter-revolution. Then he concentrated his troops and launched an attack on Wuhan. He took back Hankow and Hanyang from the revolutionaries and bombarded Wuchang across the river, seriously menacing the existence of the Wuchang Military Government. Needing an enemy to maintain his importance, Yuan did not cross the river to attack Wuchang, but launched a peace offensive against the revolutionaries.

After the Wuchang Uprising the revolutionary enthusiasm of the people all over the country soared and under the leadership and influence of the revolutionaries the new armies and secret societies launched uprisings in various provinces. By the latter part of November 1911 fifteen out of the twenty-four provinces and regions in the country had declared their independence. Apart from the frontier regions only a very small number of places were still under the direct control of the reactionary Ching government, and uprisings were also contemplated in these places. One uprising even broke out in Chihli, the province in which the central government was situated. At the same time, fierce struggles against the feudal system were waged by the peasants. In Kiangsu, Kwangtung and Hunan, for instance, many peasants, having managed to arm themselves, fought against feudal oppression and meted out punishment to the local despots and bad gentry. Peasant uprisings of different magnitudes broke out in various other provinces. The one which broke out in Szechuan was on a particular big scale. With the exception of the Taiping Heavenly Kingdom movement no peasant uprising in modern Chinese history compares with it. The people in various provinces which had become independent, especially those in Hupeh, waged heroic struggles to support the Wuchang Uprising. Countless numbers of workers and peasants, as well as intellectuals, joined the forces in revolt, and showed great heroism in the course of battle. When the revolutionary forces fought with the Ching army the broad masses of people gave them strong support and delivered telling blows against the government forces. This shows that revolutionary ideas had sunk deeply into the hearts of the people and that the Ching government had reached the point where it was no longer able to maintain its reactionary rule. Unfortunately this great revolutionary struggle lacked powerful political leadership. After the failure of the Canton Uprising on April 27, 1911, the organization of the Revolutionary League had become weak and loose-knit and it almost disintegrated after the Wuchang Uprising. In contrast the constitutional monarchists were very active. Within a short time they had wormed their way into the revolutionary camp and usurped its leadership. These monarchists became supporters of the republic overnight. In this manner many constitutional monarchists became "founders of the republic". Their presence in the revolutionary camp caused many contradictions and disputes and their presence was also the reason why, long after the Wuchang Uprising, no central leadership could be set up, in spite of the fact that the uprising was supported by many provinces. It was not until November 30 that the first meeting was held in a foreign concession of Hankow by the representatives of the various provinces which had become independent. The meeting lasted for five whole days. Nobody dared to suggest how the forces should be organized to repulse Yuan Shih-kai's attack and to push forward the revolution till it won a nation-wide victory. Those in attendance merely carried on a laboured discussion on the so-called organic law of the provisional government. Their attention was obviously focussed on the problem of how to secure official positions for themselves. What was even more strange was that at the same time Yuan Shih-kai's cannons were still roaring, the meeting passed a resolution to the effect that "if Yuan Shih-kai supported the revolution he would be elected president of the republic". This clearly shows that, even in the early stages of the revolution, they were already prepared to capitulate.

On December 2 the revolutionary forces from Kiangsu and Chekiang captured Nanking and the representatives of the different provinces decided to make Nanking the site of the provisional government. While this preparation was going on in Nanking, the various groups came together in a frantic scramble for position and power. It was only when Dr. Sun Yat-sen returned to Shanghai, at the end of December, that the situation was cleared up. Dr. Sun was elected provisional president and on January 1, 1912, the Provisional Government of the Republic of China was inaugurated. This provisional government was composed of constitutional monarchists, bureaucrats, warlords, and revolutionaries, the latter predominating. It was a bourgeois government, and it strived to realize bourgeois democracy in China, but owing to the weakness of the Chinese bourgeoisie, its realization was not possible. As a matter of fact, the Provisional Government in Nanking was never stable. After Dr. Sun Yat-sen had become provisional president, acting in accordance with a previous decision made by the representatives of the various provinces, he immediately wired Yuan Shih-kai, expressing his willingness to resign as soon as an agreement could be reached between the revolutionaries and the Ching government. As a matter of fact, the president's job was merely to preside over peace talks.

I arrived in Nanking at the beginning of 1912 when both the provisional government and the senate had been set up. When I was on my way there, the Szechuan Military Government in Chungking reached an agreement with the Great Han Military Government in Chengtu. They jointly sent Huang Fu-sheng, Li Chao-fu and Hsiung Cheng-chang to Nanking as senators from Szechuan. This obviated the necessity for Yang Shu-kan and me to represent the Szechuan Military Government of Chungking. Dr. Sun Yat-sen wanted me to work on the secretariat in the president's office. "You've come just in time," he told me. "We're now busy winding up our work and we need your help." I complied with his request. An agreement between the north and south was certain, and it was clear that as soon as it was reached the secretariat of the president's office would be abolished. The secretariat, which had been a centre of attraction for office-seekers, was now shunned by them. The secretaries began to make their own plans, some of them going right over to Yuan Shih-kai's side to get jobs. Cheng Ming-chao, an old bureaucrat, secured a high position in the secretariat after the provisional government had been set up in Nanking. Later, realizing that his job would not last long, he stopped going to the office. Another secretary, named Chin Yu-liu, filled out a certificate appointing himself magistrate in his own county of Wusih. This soon became known and was a popular joke. From what has been said we can see that in the Provisional Government of Nanking, not only the bureaucrats and politicians lacked stamina but, under their influence, even some of the revolutionaries were corrupted, gradually lost their revolutionary determination, and pursued their own selfish ends in search of official position and wealth.

21. YUAN SHIH-KAI USURPS SUPREME POWER

Owing to lack of leadership the anti-feudal struggle of the broad masses of peasants, inspired by the Revolution of 1911, did not fully develop. The Chinese bourgeoisie being very weak itself feared to arouse the peasants to take part in the revolution. The result was that under the pressure of the imperialist and feudal forces the bourgeoisie could do nothing but retreat and compromise. When Dr. Sun Yat-sen returned to China from abroad he did not consider it correct to hold peace talks with Yuan Shih-kai, although at that time, "public opinion" (that is, the public opinion of the upper social strata) was in favour of peace negotiation. The imperialists, especially the British imperialists, strongly supported Yuan Shih-kai and looked upon him as their new tool. John Jordan, then the British minister in Peking, was the chief conspirator supporting Yuan Shih-kai's attempt to strangle the revolution. It is true that the British imperialists also tried to establish connections with Dr. Sun Yat-sen but this was merely a crafty move. Because of the collaboration between Chinese and foreign reactionaries who pressed vehemently for peace negotiations, most of the powerful members of the Nanking Provisional Government disapproved of Dr. Sun Yat-sen's stand. Wang Ching-wei even asked him: "Is it because you are unwilling to lose the presidency that you disapprove of the peace negotiations?" Besieged by various people Dr. Sun Yat-sen finally gave in.

After the provisional government had been set up the peace negotiations continued. Nanking promised to elect Yuan Shih-kai president after the successful conclusion of the peace negotiations. The election was conditional on the abdication of the Ching emperor and Yuan's support for the republic. Yuan Shih-kai then forced the Ching emperor to abdicate. The peace negotiations were soon concluded. Dr. Sun Yat-sen in order to defend the republic made two proposals which he considered to be ingenious. The first was that a provisional constitution should be drawn up to keep Yuan Shih-kai within bounds by law. Secondly, Nanking should be the capital of China. The latter proposal was designed to force Yuan Shih-kai to leave Peking, the centre of the imperialist and feudal forces. In February 1912 the Nanking senate devoted a whole month to drawing up the Provisional Constitution, which later became famous in China's constitutional history. This statute followed the political practice of bourgeois countries, according to which state power was divided into three branches — legislative, judicial and executive. Yuan Shih-kai paid little attention to the Provisional Constitution because he knew that it could be discarded at any time, but he did worry about the problem of moving the capital to Nanking. In a message to the Nanking Provisional Government on February 13, notifying it of the Ching emperor's abdication Yuan Shih-kai expressed his unwillingness to go south. At the last moment Nanking again gave in and allowed Yuan to inaugurate his presidency in Peking.

Realizing that the Nanking Provisional Government would soon cease to exist many revolutionaries considered that their revolutionary ideals would never come to fruition and were deeply grieved. Many revolutionaries from Szechuan were in Nanking at that time, and after discussing the matter they decided to hold a memorial service for the revolutionary martyrs of Szechuan. This service served the dual purpose of showing respect for the martyrs and providing an opportunity to express their own sorrow. Dr. Sun Yat-sen was present at the service. After holding the service we petitioned the authorities to confer posthumous honours on the martyrs, and some other provinces followed our example.

Having paid our respect to the dead we considered our own problems. We members of the secretariat were determined not to work under Yuan Shih-kai. Some wanted to bring out a newspaper so that they could fight against Yuan Shih-kai, using their pens as swords. Others proposed that we go abroad again to finish our interrupted studies, a suggestion which won general approval. Tsai Yuan-pei, a member of the Revolutionary League, was then the Minister of Education in the provisional government and, with his sanction, many revolutionaries were allowed to study abroad with government aid. One after another they left China for foreign countries. Many well intentioned people among them thought that, the republic having been founded, they might contribute to the country's national construction if they acquired some real training. They did not know that although the Ching government had been overthrown by the Revolution of 1911, Yuan Shih-kai, its successor, was also a tool of the imperialist and feudal forces. Nor did they anticipate that after China became a republic, not only would it fail to prosper but it would flounder more deeply in a quagmire of national crisis and calamities. Although I was included in those who had the privilege of studying abroad with government aid, I did not sail immediately, because I still had some unfinished work to complete.

22. MY RETURN TO SZECHUAN

With the resignation of Dr. Sun Yat-sen and the investiture of Yuan Shih-kai it was obvious that the Revolution of 1911 had practically failed. China remained a semi-colonial and semi-feudal country with imperialism and feudalism, like two huge mountains, still oppressing its people. Many revolutionaries did not seem to be aware of this fact. They still cherished illusions about Yuan Shih-kai and the imperialists. In August 1912 Dr. Sun Yat-sen was invited to Peking by

Yuan Shih-kai. Yuan gave him a sumptuous reception, and went to great lengths to please him. He succeeded in hood-winking Dr. Sun Yat-sen who said, "Yuan is the only man who can rule China today." He accepted an appointment as the director-general of railways and planned to build 100,000 kilometres of railways as a means of realizing his hope for the salvation of China through industrialization. He even paid a visit to Japan to achieve this end, but it did not take him long to realize that his dream had been smashed to smithereens.

After the conclusion of the peace negotiations between the north and south I went to Peking. One day, a friend came to me and said he had read in a newspaper that Yuan Shih-kai wanted to appoint me as his special commissioner to convey his goodwill to the people of Szechuan. I was very surprised. I immediately went to see Chu Fei-huang, a member of the Revolutionary League from Szechuan who had become Yuan's protege, suspecting that he had something to do with the matter. Chu said, "The president has been trying to get in touch with you. He wanted both of us to return to Szechuan under the title of special commissioner to mediate between the Chengtu and Chungking parties." I said, "Szechuan is our home province. How can we go back to our own people with such a title? Besides, while I was working in the secretariat of the Nanking Provisional Government I made a pledge to my colleagues that I would never again assume any official post." Seeing that I was firm, Yuan Shih-kai finally agreed not to give me any title but still wanted me to go with Chu Fei-huang to Szechuan to tell the people there of the "government's concern" about them and to work for the unification of the province. At that time I did not realize that Yuan wanted to use me for the purpose of helping him fulfil the task of unifying Szechuan, because he was quite sure that Chu's prestige alone was insufficient. I only thought that it would be a service to the people of the province if Szechuan could be unified and freed from calamities. Feeling it was a duty I should not evade, I complied with Yuan's request.

During the summer of 1912 I went back to Szechuan with Chu Fei-huang. An agreement had already been reached between Chungking and Chengtu, which, like the one reached in the north-south peace negotiations, meant the capitulation of Chungking to Chengtu, that is, the capitulation of the revolutionary forces to the forces of reaction. Yang Wei was then the commissioner of military police. He was one of the six leaders of the Chengtu Uprising who were arrested in 1907. Believing Yang Wei to be a man of ability I urged Chu Fei-huang to use both our names to wire Yuan Shih-kai, recommending Yang as the garrison commander of Chengtu. Yuan immediately appointed him to the post and raised him to the rank of lieutenant-general. Yuan of course only did this to humour the revolutionaries, but the reactionaries, feeling uneasy, immediately enlisted the help of Yuan's favourites to persuade Yuan to revoke the appointment. Although Yuan did not do this, his tacit withdrawal of support made it impossible for Yang to assume the post. Yuan, seeing that I was still intent on working for the revolution, hastily wired me to return to Peking. I was at home in Junghsien when I received the telegram and left at once for Peking with Chu Fei-huang.

Acting in the name of the Association for Economical Study in France, I had succeeded in helping a number of young people to study in France during my stay in Szechuan. The association had been organized by Li Shih-tseng and other anarchists. Although these men had subsequently degenerated into reactionaries and become Yuan Shih-kai's henchmen, it should be said that by sending a number of students to study sciences in France, the association did contribute something beneficial. The real aim of Li Shih-tseng and others like him in organizing this association was not to help the students, but to use it as a means whereby they might become known as famous educationalists. During the First World War the name

138

of the association was changed into the "Association for Study Through Work in France" and many more students were sent to study there. The more progressive ones later became leading members of the Chinese Communist Party, such as Chou En-lai, Teng Hsiao-ping, Chen Yi, Li Fu-chun and Nieh Jung-chen, and martyrs of the Chinese Communist Party, such as Chao Shih-yen, Chen Yen-nien and Wang Jo-fei.

When I arrived in Peking, the members of the Revolutionary League headed by Sung Chiao-jen had already reorganized the league and changed its name to the Kuomintang in order to take part in the parliamentary election which was being manipulated by Yuan Shih-kai. It was Sung Chiao-jen's belief that if the Kuomintang could gain a majority of seats in parliament and form a cabinet, the Chinese Republic would become a really democratic, permanently peaceful country and that Yuan Shih-kai would be president in name only. He even admitted many old-style politicians and feudal remnants into the party, in order to gain a large number of votes for Kuomintang candidates. He tried to make the party programme more acceptable to them and, defying the opposition of many league members, stripped it of all revolutionary ideas. "Equalization of landownership" became "the policy of paying attention to the people's livelihood" and "strive to gain international equality" became "support international peace". In other words, the anti-imperialist and anti-feudal content of the programme of the Revolutionary League was entirely eliminated. Even the article on "equality between men and women" was deleted, to the annoyance and opposition of the women comrades. Tang Chun-ying, one of the women members of the Revolutionary League who had led a northern expeditionary team immediately after the capture of Nanking during the Revolution of 1911, raised objections and challenged Sung Chiao-jen when she heard that he had struck out the article on "equality between men and women".

Towards the end of 1912 the parliamentary elections began. Sung Chiao-jen made speeches in many places just as was done in Western "democratic" countries. Later, when victory was scored in the elections he was flushed with joy, and proclaimed his political views everywhere he went. While he was still dizzy with success Yuan Shih-kai prepared a trap for him. On March 20, 1913, he was assassinated at the railway station in Shanghai. While breathing his last, he still expressed the hope that Yuan Shih-kai would be "honest and frank", unaware that Yuan was responsible for his assassination.

With Sung Chiao-jen's death, the revolutionaries' illusions were shattered. They had no alternative but to hurriedly wage a struggle against Yuan Shih-kai.

23. THE FAILURE OF THE SECOND REVOLUTION AND THE CONTINUED PURSUIT OF TRUTH

Everybody knew the political cause of Sung Chiao-jen's death. Yuan Shih-kai pretended that he had nothing to do with it, and ordered "a thorough investigation of the case" stating that he would "punish the criminal with great severity". The truth was soon revealed that it was Yuan Shih-kai himself who had sent the assassin. His plot having been exposed, Yuan decided to continue with his plans. Ignoring legal procedure and without the approval of the senate, he obtained a huge loan from the imperialist powers, expanded his army and prepared to wipe out the revolutionary forces which opposed him in the various provinces.

In April 1913, Yuan Shih-kai borrowed the sum of 25 million pounds from the Five-Power Consortium which was organized by Britain, France, Germany, Japan and tsarist Russia. It was known as the "rehabilitation" loan. Meanwhile he was busy transferring his troops and making preparations to attack Kiangsi and the other provinces still under the control of the revolutionary forces. Yuan then dismissed three Kuomintang governors from office — Li Lieh-chun, governor of

Kiangsi, Pai Wen-wei, governor of Anhwei, and Hu Han-min, governor of Kwangtung, under the pretext that they opposed the loan and were defiant of the central government. In July he issued an order for a punitive expedition against the troops commanded by Kuomintang officers.

Dr. Sun Yat-sen had returned to Shanghai from Japan in March, just before the assassination of Sung Chiao-jen and was furious. He decided to organize a punitive expedition against Yuan Shih-kai to carry out a second revolution. To oppose Yuan I left Peking for Shanghai. When the "rehabilitation" loan was contracted it was rumoured that Yuan was going to change the Kuomintang governors of Kwangtung, Kiangsi, Anhwei and Hunan. I therefore proposed to Dr. Sun Yat-sen that the four governors should make the first move and issue a joint statement against Yuan's violation of the law, declaring that they would accept no further orders from him until a legal government was established. Dr. Sun agreed with my proposal but Huang Hsing did not. He said that if my proposal was carried out it would expose his preparations for military action against Yuan. In reality Yuan knew that the Kuomintang opposed him just as the Kuomintang knew Yuan's opposition to it. All this was an open secret. Yuan made the first move, dismissed the Kuomintang governors from their office, which left the anti-Yuan struggle in an unfavourable position.

On July 12 Li Lieh-chun, governor of Kiangsi, declared independence in Hukow, Kiangsi, and organized a punitive expedition against Yuan. He was supported in this by the provinces of Kiangsu, Anhwei, Kwangtung and Szechuan. Yuan concentrated his army for an attack on Hukow and defeated Li Lieh-chun's troops. In less than two months the struggles against Yuan had all subsided. The main reason for the quick failure of the second revolution was that, after the Revolution of 1911, the Kuomintang had abandoned its revolutionary programme and gradually alienated itself from

141

the masses. Consequently when the anti-Yuan struggle was launched, the Kuomintang no longer enjoyed the warm support of the masses as it had done in the days of the Revolutionary League.

The anti-Yuan banner was also raised in Szechuan. Yuan issued an order for my arrest, thinking that I was the instigator of this struggle. Being forced to go abroad again, at the end of 1913 I set out for France.

Previous to my departure, Jen Hung-nien, one of my friends, who was a member of the Revolutionary League, committed suicide in Hangchow. He killed himself because he was angry and disheartened. He saw that Yuan Shih-kai, like the Ching government, was ruining the country and bringing disaster to the people, and that all his hopes for the revolution were lost. It was at this time that Yuan Shih-kai ordered my arrest. When my elder brother, who had become blind and was suffering both sickness and poverty in Chengtu, heard about my threatened arrest he lost hope and felt that there was no future for our home and country. He also committed suicide by hanging himself. The Revolution of 1911 had indeed brought a ray of light to the age-long darkness of China. It brought joy and encouragement to the people, but, in a short time, Yuan Shih-kai usurped state power, and threw the whole nation into a dark abyss again. The people's disappointment and despair was so great that a number of them committed suicide. Personally I have always been against the idea of committing suicide. I believe that it is unwise for a man to kill himself because if he has courage enough to sacrifice his life it is far better for him to go and fight his enemy and risk death that way. In addition, I have always been extremely optimistic with regard to the future of our motherland. It is my belief that our great country, which has a glorious history of several thousand years and hundreds of millions of industrious and courageous people, can certainly break through the veil of darkness and launch itself into a bright and splendid future. Nevertheless, I could not but feel disturbed about the dangers and difficulties the country was facing, the sacrifices made by many comrades, and the suicide of my brother and friends. On my way to France, standing alone on the deck of the steamer, looking at the rolling waves of the boundless ocean, I felt the blood surge through my veins. Oh! Dear Motherland, I said to myself, when will you throw off your heavy chains and be liberated?

Quite by chance the ship on which I journeyed to France was a Japanese liner on which I passed the New Year's Day of 1914. The Chinese national flag was missing from the international flags hung on the ship during the New Year Day celebrations and I felt extremely indignant. I suggested that the Chinese passengers lodge a protest with the captain, although all we could expect from him, at best, would be an apology. I recalled that ten years previously, when I was studying in the Seijo School, a struggle was waged in regard to the hanging of national flags during a New Year celebration. Who could have known then that ten years later China would still be as ignored in the eyes of the world? Was this the result of ten long years of hard revolutionary work? Could it be that we had taken the wrong path, used the wrong methods of work? I was determined to find the answer to these questions, and eagerly sought the truth that would bring salvation to the country and my people.

Finally I struck on the truth which would really bring salvation to the country and people. It was the universally applicable truth that makes it possible for the working people to seek their own emancipation — Marxism-Leninism. The victory of the October Revolution in 1917 illuminated the correct road for the people of the whole world. It was under the resplendent light of the October Revolution that in 1919 the May 4 Movement was launched in China, and that in 1921 the Chinese Communist Party was founded. It was under

143

the correct leadership of the Chinese Communist Party and its leader Mao Tse-tung that the Chinese people began the New-Democratic Revolution and won their great victory. Following the leadership of Mao Tse-tung I was able to see the people win their victory and to share their happiness.

POSTSCRIPT

Fifty years have passed since the Revolution of 1911. Fifty years is quite a long period of time in the life of an individual but it is but an instant in the history of mankind. In the fifty years since 1911, China has undergone radical changes. The Chinese people have overthrown the reactionary rule of the Ching emperor, the northern warlords and the Kuomintang. They have undergone the old-democratic revolution, carried out the New-Democratic Revolution and completed, in the main, the Socialist Revolution, thus enabling China to change from a semi-colonial, semi-feudal society into a socialist one through the stage of a new-democratic society. In only half a century China has traversed a path which took other countries hundreds of years. An extremely beautiful vista is now unfolding before us. What great joy it is for us and what pride we have in being citizens of our great motherland! But looking back on the past, we cannot help but feel that victory has its price. What hardships the forerunners of the revolution suffered! To end the suffering of the Chinese people, how many bitter struggles were waged and how much blood was shed by these heroic and noble-spirited people. Thoughts of the bitter past make us treasure our happy present and make us determined to make greater effort to ensure a bright future. I have struggled for a strong and prosperous motherland for the past sixty years. Now that the situation facing us is exceedingly favourable, in spite of my age, I cannot help feeling stronger than ever and more eager to march forward. As long as I am living, together with my younger comrades, I will use the last ounce of my energy to help build up my motherland into an extremely prosperous and strong socialist country and to realize man's greatest and noblest ideal — that of communism.

ABOUT THE AUTHOR

Wu Yu-chang, the author of this book, is one of the oldest living revolutionaries in China. He is popularly known as Wu Lao or Wu the Elder, a name carrying love and respect.

China was under the rule of the Ching, its last feudal dynasty, when the author was born 85 years ago. The government was corrupt, the danger of foreign aggression was growing, and the people were forced to endure great privation and suffering. Internal and external troubles weighed heavily on everyone. As he grew up young Wu Yu-chang fervently sought for a way of national salvation like all the progressive intellectuals of his day. At one time he was influenced by bourgeois reformist ideas but he soon saw that salvation was not to be found in that way. Later he took part in the Revolution of 1911, the bourgeois democratic revolution led by the revolutionary democrat Sun Yat-sen. When this revolution ended in failure, Wu Lao found himself standing at the crossroads. After a long period of deep searching for the truth, he reached the conclusion that only the application of the doctrine of Marxism-Leninism could save his people and country. He was 47 years of age when he became a Marxist-Leninist and a fighter in the vanguard of the proletariat. The present book contains an account of his struggle before his forty-seventh year.

Wu Yu-chang is now a member of the Central Committee of the Chinese Communist Party, a member of the Standing Committee of the National People's Congress, and president of the China People's University.

辛 亥 革 命

——中国近代史上一次伟大的民主革命

吴玉章　著

*

外文出版社出版（北京）

1962年第一版

1964年第三版

（译文修订本）

编号．（英）11050—22

00150（精）

00110（平）

11—E—525